Faith to Live By

DEREK PRINCE

FAITH TO LIVE BY

Servant Books
Ann Arbor, Michigan

CGM Publishing
Ft. Lauderdale, Florida

Unless otherwise indicated, all Scripture quotations in this book are taken
from the New American Standard Bible, © the Lockman Foundation 1960,
1962, 1963, 1968, 1971, 1972, 1973, 1975 and are used by permission.

Scripture quotations identified NEB are from the New English Bible, copyright © The Delegates of the Oxford University Press and the Syndics of the
Cambridge University Press, 1961 and 1970. Reprinted by permission.

Scripture quotations identified NIV are from the New International Version
New Testament copyright © 1973 New York Bible Society International.
Reprinted by permission.

Scripture quotations identified KJV are from the King James Version of
the Bible.

Printed in the United States of America

ISBN 0-89283-042-5

"To all who treasure the same faith as ourselves, given through the righteousness of our God and savior Jesus Christ."

2 Peter 1:1
(Jerusalem Bible)

CONTENTS

Chapter One

Faith vs. Sight

FAITH!

Who can fully measure or express the potential represented by that short, simple word—FAITH?

Perhaps the clearest way to bring faith's potential into focus is to set side by side two statements made by Jesus:

> With God *all things are possible* (Matthew 19:26).
> *All things are possible* to him who believes (Mark 9:23).

In each of these statements we find the words "all things are possible." In the first passage they are applied to God; in the second they are applied to the one who believes. It is not too difficult, perhaps, to accept that all things are possible with God. Can we equally accept that all things are possible to the one who believes? Yet this is what Jesus tells us.

In practical terms, what does this mean? It means that, through faith, the things that are possible to God are made equally possible to the one who believes. Faith is the channel that makes God's possibilities available to us. Through faith, all that is possible to God becomes equally possible to us. No wonder that, from beginning to end, the Bible consistently emphasizes the unique and supreme importance of faith.

Problems of Translation

Before we go further with our study of faith, it will be helpful to clear up a linguistic misunderstanding that often causes difficulties for people who approach the New Testament through an English translation. In English we have two different words: a noun, *faith;* a verb, to *believe.* In origin or form, there is no obvious connection between these two words. As a result, preachers sometimes seek to make a distinction between "believing" and "having faith." However, there is no basis for this distinction in the original Greek of the New Testament.

In Greek the word for "faith" is *pistis* and the word for "believe" is *pisteuo.* The verb is formed directly from the noun: faith, *pistis;* I believe, *pisteuo.* The stem of each word is made up of the same four letters—*pist.* As far as the Bible is concerned, believing is exercising faith. Conversely, exercising faith is believing.

When we turn to the words that express the opposite of faith, we again find a difference between English and Greek. In English the opposite of "faith" is "unbelief." We have no such word as "unfaith." But in Greek there is a direct connection between faith and its opposite. "Faith" is *pistis;* "unbelief" is *apistia.* (In Greek the negative prefix "a" corresponds to the English prefix "un.") The same four-letter stem *pist* occurs in both Greek words: faith, *pistis;* unbelief, *apistia.*

Also connected with this four-letter stem *pist,* we

have the adjective *pistos*—faithful, believing. From this, the negative prefix "a" gives us the opposite adjective, *apistos*—unfaithful, unbelieving.

For the sake of clarity, we will set these five words side by side in two parallel columns:

	Greek	English
Noun:	*pist*is	faith
Noun:	a*pist*ia	unbelief
Adjective:	*pist*os	faithful, believing
Adjective:	a*pist*os	unfaithful, unbelieving
Verb:	*pist*euo	I believe

We see that all five Greek words are visibly linked by the stem form *pist* that occurs in each of them. Altogether, they occur almost 600 times in the original text of the New Testament. On this basis alone, it is clear that these words represent a theme that is central to the Bible's total revelation.

Faith Defined

The eleventh chapter of Hebrews deals exclusively with the theme of faith. Its opening verse provides us with a definition of faith as the term is used in the Bible.

> Now faith is the substance* of things hoped for, the conviction of things not seen.

This verse tells us two main things about faith. First, "faith is the *substance* of things hoped for." Faith is so real that it is actually called a substance. The Greek word is *hupostasis.* It means literally "that which stands

*"Substance" is the alternative given in the margin for "assurance" and it better expresses the literal meaning.

under" something else or "provides the basis for" something else.

The same word *hupostasis* occurs in Hebrews 1:3 where we are told that Jesus is "the exact representation of the Father's *nature.*" The word here translated "nature" is *hupostasis.* The meaning is that God the Father is the eternal, invisible, underlying reality of which Jesus Christ, the Son, is the visible expression. Applying this to Hebrews 11:1, we may say that faith is the "underlying reality" of things hoped for. Faith is real; faith is a substance.

Secondly, faith is "the *conviction* of things not seen." Other translations say, "the *evidence* of things not seen." Whichever translation we prefer, the vital point is that faith deals with things we cannot see. Faith relates to the *invisible.*

Two verses further on, in Hebrews 11:3, the writer again stresses faith's relationship to the invisible:

By faith we understand that the worlds were prepared by the word of God, so that what is seen was not made out of things which are visible.

The writer here points a contrast between "what is seen" and "things which are not visible," between the visible and the invisible. Our senses relate us to the visible world, to "what is seen." But faith takes us behind the visible to the invisible—to the underlying reality by which the whole universe was formed: that is, the word of God.

Thus, faith relates to two eternal, invisible realities: to God Himself and to His word. Biblical faith has only these two objects. In secular speech, of course, we speak of faith in many other contexts. We can talk about having faith in a newspaper, or in a medicine, or in a political leader. But faith is not used that way in the Bible. In the Bible, faith is related solely and exclusively to two things we cannot see with the natural eye: first to God, and second to God's word.

By Faith, Not by Sight

The opposition between faith and sight is brought out by Paul in 2 Corinthians 5:7: "for we walk by faith, not by sight." If we walk by sight, we do not need faith. If we walk by faith, we do not need sight. Each excludes the other.

This is contrary to our natural way of thinking. The world says, "Seeing is believing." But the Bible reverses the order: First we must believe, then we will see. This principle is so important that we will look at some passages of Scripture that illustrate it. In Psalm 27:13 David says, "I would have despaired unless I had believed that I would see the goodness of the LORD in the land of the living." Which came first, believing or seeing? Believing. What was true for David is true for all of us. If we cannot believe that we will see the goodness of the Lord, we will despair. The thing that keeps us from despairing is not what we see but what we believe.

This agrees with the statement made about Moses in Hebrews 11:27: "By faith he left Egypt, not fearing the wrath of the king; for he endured, as seeing Him who is unseen." Nothing in Moses' visible circumstances at this time could give him any hope or encouragement. But in spite of all that was against him, he "endured" because he was able to "see the unseen." How did he do this? By *faith*. Faith enables us to "see the unseen" and thus to endure when the visible world offers us no hope or encouragement.

Again, we turn to the record of Jesus raising Lazarus from the dead in John chapter 11. In verses 39–40 we read:

> (39)   Jesus said, "Remove the stone." Martha, the sister of the deceased, said to Him, "Lord, by this time there will be a stench; for he has been dead four days."
>
> (40)   Jesus said to her, "Did I not say to you, if you believe, you will see the glory of God?"

What Jesus asks here of Martha, He asks of all who desire to see the glory of God. We must "believe that we will see." We do not see first, then believe. We believe first; then—as a result of believing—we see. Faith comes before sight.

Here, then, is the basic conflict between the old nature and the new nature. The old nature demands to *see* since the old nature lives by the senses. God has to deliver us from that old nature and that old way of life and bring us to a new nature and a new way of life which says, "I'm content *not* to see. I don't walk by sight but by faith."

In 2 Corinthians 4:17–18 we are challenged yet once more by the contrast between the visible and the invisible:

> (17)   For momentary, light affliction is producing for us an eternal weight of glory far beyond all comparison,
>
> (18)   while we look not at the things which are seen, but at the things which are not seen; for the things which are seen are temporal,

but the things which are not seen are eternal.

Paul's language here contains a deliberate paradox. He speaks about "looking at things which are not seen." How can we do this? There is only one way—by faith!

There is great significance in the word *"while"*: "while we look not at the things which are seen." It stresses the same lesson that Moses learned in his test of endurance. In the providence of God, affliction serves a useful purpose for the believer. It forms and strengthens our character and prepares us for the eternal glory that lies ahead. *But affliction serves us only while we keep our eyes on the invisible realm.* If we lose sight of this and become preoccupied with the world of time and of the senses, we are no longer able to receive the benefits that affliction is intended to work out for us.

So we are caught between two worlds, the temporal and the eternal. The temporal is that which we can see; we contact it with our senses. But the eternal is the world God wants us at home in. And we can be at home in that world by only one means: faith. Faith is the *one* thing that relates us to the unseen realities of God and His word.

Summary

Faith lifts us above the realm of our own ability and makes God's possibilities available to us.

Faith relates us to two unseen realities: God and His word. As we maintain this relationship to God through faith, we are enabled to endure and to overcome the tests and the hardships that confront us in our daily life. These in turn become opportunities for God to reveal His goodness and His glory.

There is an ongoing tension between faith and sight. Our old nature is at home in the world of the senses and it demands to "see." As Christians, we need to cultivate the new nature that is prepared to trust God and His word without demanding other evidence.

Chapter Two

Faith vs. Hope

In chapter 1 we examined the difference between faith and sight—between believing and seeing. In this chapter we will examine the difference between *faith* and *hope.* Herein lies one of the greatest sources of misunderstanding among Christians today. Many Christians are disappointed and frustrated in prayer because they do not receive what they think they should. Often it is because they are praying in hope, but not in faith. The results promised by God to faith are not promised to hope.

What is the difference? How can we distinguish faith from hope?

Faith Is in the Heart

The first main difference is that faith is in the *heart,* while hope is in the *mind.* In Romans 10:10 Paul says, "For *with the heart* man believeth *unto* righteousness " (KJV). True biblical faith originates in the heart. Expressed by the verb to *believe,* it is followed by the preposition *unto,* indicating the result which it produces—"unto righteousness." "Unto" implies motion or transition of some kind. Faith is never static. It always expresses itself in motion, change, activity. A person who truly believes will be changed by what he believes.

On the other hand, a person who merely accepts truth with his intellect can remain unchanged by it. Mental acceptance of truth is not faith. To produce faith, truth must penetrate beyond the conscious mind into the inner center and source of life which is called the heart. Truth received intellectually by the mind may be sterile and ineffective, but truth received by faith into the heart is always dynamic and life-changing in its outworking.

In Proverbs 4:23 Solomon warns us, "Watch over your heart with all diligence, For from it flow the springs of life." Everything that finally decides the course of our life proceeds out of our heart. True biblical faith proceeds from the heart and determines the way we live. It is not a mere intellectual concept, entertained by the mind; it is a real, active force at work in the heart.

However, God does not leave our mind without its proper provision. Faith at work in the heart produces hope in the mind. This follows from the definition of faith that we have already examined in Hebrews 11:1: "Faith is the substance of things hoped for . . . " Faith in the heart is the substance—the underlying reality. This provides a valid, scriptural basis for the hope that we entertain in our mind.

In 1 Thessalonians 5:8 Paul mentions the different areas of our personality affected respectively by faith and by hope: "But since we are of the day, let us be sober, having put on the breastplate of faith and love, and as a helmet, the hope of salvation." Faith and love are the breastplate, and the breastplate protects the heart. Hope is the helmet and it protects the head, or the mind.

In distinguishing faith from hope, we do not mean to belittle hope. Hope, in the biblical sense, is a confident expectation of good—a steady, persistent optimism. It is this which protects our minds. Every Christian should wear this helmet of hope 24 hours a day. If we lay aside the helmet and begin to dwell on negative thoughts and gloomy forebodings, our minds are vulnerable to Satan's subtle attacks.

Christian optimism of this kind is not fanciful or unrealistic. It is not mere wishful thinking. It must be based firmly and exclusively on the statements and promises of Scripture. For example, in Romans 8:28 we are told, "And we know that God causes all things to work together for good to those who love God, to those who are called according to His purpose." If God is working all things together for our good, what room is left for anything but optimism?

However, in applying this verse to our lives, we first need to check that we are meeting the conditions which it implies. Do we truly love God? Are we seeking to fulfill His purpose for our lives? If so, then God is working all things—every event, every situation—together for our good. This leaves only one attitude of mind that we can logically adopt: optimism. In the light of this, for a Christian to be a pessimist is, in fact, a denial of his faith.

This example confirms what has already been said: faith is the only solid basis for hope. We must first truly believe what Romans 8:28 tells us—that all things are working together for our good. If we believe this, we have no alternative but hope. But if we do not believe it, then our hope has no solid basis.

It follows from what has been said that there are two

forms of hope, outwardly similar but different in one vital respect. The first form of hope is based on genuine faith in the heart and it is therefore valid. Its expectation will, in due time, be fulfilled. The second form of hope is in the mind alone, lacking any basis of genuine faith in the heart, and therefore has no scriptural validity. More likely than not, its expectation is doomed to disappointment. Until we have learned to distinguish between these two forms of hope, we are always in danger of entertaining hopes which will go unfulfilled.

Faith Is in the Present

The second main difference between faith and hope is that faith is in the present and hope is in the future. Faith is a *substance,* something that is already here; hope is an *expectation,* something that necessarily looks toward the future.

I cannot tell how many people, in the years of my ministry, have come to me and said, "I have great faith; pray for me." I remember one man who said, "I have all the faith in the world." I thought, facetiously, that this was rather unfair because it left none for the rest of us! Seriously, every time I hear people say, "I have great faith," my heart sinks because my experience tells me they will not get what they claim they have faith for. They may be perfectly sincere, but their desires will go unanswered because they have confused faith with hope.

It is very easy to do this because, as we have already seen, hope is in the mind while faith is in the heart. We usually know well enough what is in our mind, but it is much harder to know what is in our heart. We have a strong expectation in our mind and we mistakenly call it faith, but it is really hope. Lacking the necessary basis of faith, we do not see the results we expected.

There is an unpredictable quality about faith which mirrors the unpredictable nature of the human heart. Sometimes I have "felt" that I had strong faith, but nothing has happened. At other times I have not "felt" any faith and yet I have been pleasantly surprised at what God has done. The kind of faith I can "feel" is usually mental—a substitute for true heart faith. On the other hand, there can at times come forth out of my heart true, effective faith that I did not know was there—with results that amaze me!

Many people who say, "I believe God will heal me," really mean, "I hope He'll heal me tomorrow." That is not faith because faith is not for tomorrow; faith is something that we have now. If we keep directing our expectation toward the future, we are substituting hope for faith.

Years ago when I was a student at Cambridge, the University gave me a grant to go to Athens for my studies in Greek antiquity. I soon lost interest in the statues and monuments of Greece and became much more interested in the people living in Greece today. A friend from the University traveled with me and every morning when we stepped outside our hotel a group of shoeshine boys was waiting, determined to polish our shoes. If you have never traveled in a Mediterranean country, you have no idea of the determination of shoeshine boys. They will not accept "no" for an answer. For the first two or three days when we ventured outside our hotel we tried saying "Ochi!" throwing our heads backward with a scornful air at the same time. That is the Greek way of saying "No!" But it just didn't work; the boys shined our shoes anyway.

About the fourth day my friend tried a different tactic. The next time we walked outside our hotel door the boys approached us to shine our shoes, as usual. This time my friend looked them squarely in the face and said, "Avrio." They hesitated for a moment and we were able to pass. Can you guess what "Avrio" means? It means "Tomorrow!"

Years later, after I had become a Christian, I recalled this incident. It illustrates so vividly the way the devil sometimes cheats us as Christians. When we are seeking healing for ourselves, or praying for the salvation of an unsaved loved one, the devil does not flatly say we will not obtain what we are seeking. He does not say, "You will not be healed," or "Your loved one will not be saved." If he did that, we would not listen to him. Instead he says, "Yes, you will obtain what you are seeking, but not today; tomorrow!" And so we never come to the moment of positively apprehending that which we are seeking. We are willing to accept the devil's "Tomorrow," when we would never accept his "No!" We have hope, but not faith.

But God does not put us off until tomorrow. He says, *"Now* is 'THE ACCEPTABLE TIME,' behold *now* is 'THE DAY OF SALVATION' " (2 Corinthians 6:2). God lives in the eternal *now.* To faith He never reveals Himself as "I was" or "I will be," but always as "I am." When faith contacts God, it is always in the present.

When we apply this principle to the making of our petitions to God, it will revolutionize this aspect of our prayer life. In Mark 11:24 Jesus tells us, "Therefore I say to you, all things for which you pray and ask, believe that you *have received* them, and they shall be granted you." When does Jesus tell us to receive what we pray for? At some undetermined point in the future? No—but at the very moment that we pray. We "ask" and at the same moment we "receive." Thereafter we know that the things we asked for "shall be granted us."

"Granting" still remains in the future, but "receiving"—by faith—takes place when we pray. Having received now by faith, we know that, at God's appointed time, the things we received at the moment of praying will actually be granted us. Faith to receive is in the present; the manifestation of that which we receive is in the future. But without present faith there is no assurance of future manifestation.

In Hebrews 4:3 the writer puts the act of believing one stage further back in time—to the perfect tense: "For we who *have believed* enter that rest . . . ." Believing is here viewed as something already accomplished which does not need to be repeated. Having believed in this way, we "enter that rest." There is no more struggle or anxiety. We know that the thing which we have *received* by faith will in due course be *manifested* in experience. The receiving is our part of the transaction; the manifesting is God's.

Summary

Faith and hope are closely related, yet there are two important differences between them, First, faith springs from the *heart;* but hope is entertained in the *mind.* Second, faith is in the *present*—it is a substance—something we already have; but hope is directed toward the *future,* an expectation of things to come.

Hopes that are based on true faith in the heart will not be disappointed. But without this basis there is no assurance that our hopes will be fulfilled.

Hope is God's appointed protection for our minds, but it will not obtain for us those results which God has promised only to faith. The key to obtaining our petitions from God is to appropriate them, by faith, at the very moment we make them. Doing this sets us free from continuing struggle and anxiety and brings us into an inner rest.

Chapter Three

Faith as a Gift

Faith, as depicted in the New Testament, has various aspects. Its essential nature always agrees with the definition given in Hebrews 11:1—"the substance of things hoped for, the conviction of things not seen." However, this nature expresses itself in a variety of distinct but related forms.

The three main forms of faith may be defined as follows:

1. Faith to live by
2. Faith as a gift
3. Faith as a fruit

The first form of faith is a continuing personal relationship linking the believer directly to God and affecting every area of his life. It provides the motivation, the direction, and the enabling for everything he does. It is, in fact, both the sole and the sufficient ground for righteous living. For this reason we call it "faith to live by."

From chapter 5 onwards in this book, we will thoroughly examine this form of faith. But first, in this chapter, we will examine the nature of faith as a *gift*.

Then, in the next chapter, we will examine the nature of faith as a *fruit*.

The Nature of Spiritual Gifts

In 1 Corinthians chapter 12, Paul deals with the gifts of the Holy Spirit. He opens the chapter with the statement, "Now concerning spiritual gifts, brethren, I do not want you to be unaware." Then in verses 7-11 he lists nine distinct gifts:

(7)   But to each one is given the manifestation of the Spirit for the common good.

(8)   For to one is given the word of wisdom through the Spirit, and to another the word of knowledge according to the same Spirit;

(9)   to another faith by the same Spirit, and to another gifts of healing by the one Spirit,

(10)   and to another the effecting of miracles, and to another prophecy, and to another the distinguishing of spirits, to another various kinds of tongues, and to another the interpretation of tongues.

(11)   But one and the same Spirit works all these things, distributing to each one individually just as He wills.

The key word that explains the distinctive nature of these gifts is "manifestation." The Holy Spirit Himself, dwelling in a believer, is invisible. But by these gifts operating through a believer, the presence of the Holy Spirit is made manifest to human senses. In each case the results produced are within the realm of the senses; they can be seen or heard or felt.

Since these gifts are manifestations, not of the

believer's own personality, but of the Person of the Holy Spirit within the believer, all of them are supernatural in character. In every case, the results which they produce are on a higher level than the believer could ever achieve solely by his own ability. Each of them is possible only through a direct supernatural operation of the Holy Spirit. By these gifts, and through the believer, the Holy Spirit comes forth out of the invisible spiritual realm and makes a direct impact upon the physical world of space and time.

Paul establishes two important practical points concerning these gifts. First, they are distributed solely at the discretion of the Holy Spirit, according to His sovereign purposes for the ministry of each believer. Human will or achievement are not the basis for receiving these spiritual gifts. Secondly, they are given "to each one . . . for the common good"—for a useful, practical purpose. As Bob Mumford has said, the gifts of the Spirit are tools, not toys.

It has often been pointed out that these nine gifts fall naturally into three groups of three:

Three gifts of *utterance*—gifts that operate through the believer's vocal organs: prophecy; tongues; and interpretation of tongues.

Three gifts of *revelation*—gifts that impart spiritual illumination: the word of wisdom; the word of knowledge; and distinguishing of spirits.

Three gifts of *power*—gifts that demonstrate God's supernatural power in the physical realm: faith; the gifts of healing; and the effecting of miracles.

"Have God's Faith"

The gift of faith, which we will now study, is the first of the three gifts of power. It is distinguished from the other forms of faith by the fact that it is a sovereign, supernatural manifestation of the Holy Spirit working through the believer. The two key words are *sovereign* and *supernatural.*

In Matthew chapter 21 and in Mark chapter 11 we read how Jesus, on his way into Jerusalem with His disciples, came to a fig tree by the wayside. Jesus was seeking fruit. When he found that the tree contained leaves only, but no fruit, He pronounced a curse upon it, saying, "May no one ever eat fruit from you again!" (Mark 11:14). Next day, as they passed the same tree, the disciples were astonished to see that, within 24 hours, it had withered from the roots up. "Rabbi, behold," Peter commented, "the fig tree which You cursed has withered" (Mark 11:21).

To Peter's comment Jesus replied, "Have faith in God" (Mark 11:22). This is the normal English translation. However, what Jesus actually said, in its most literal form, was "Have God's faith." This brings out the special kind of faith we are speaking of here—that is, faith as a *gift.* Faith has its origin not in man, but in God. It is an aspect of God's own eternal nature. (In the last chapter of this book we shall examine this more fully.) Through the gift of faith, the Holy Spirit imparts a portion of God's own faith, directly and supernaturally, to the believer. This is faith on a divine level, as high above mere human faith as heaven is above earth.

In saying, "Have God's faith," Jesus challenged His disciples to receive and exercise this kind of faith, just as He Himself had done. He went on to tell them that with faith of this kind they would not only be able to do what they had seen Him do to the fig tree, but by speaking a word they would be able to move a mountain: "Truly I say to you, if you have faith, and do not doubt, you shall not only do what was done to the fig tree, but even if you say to this mountain, 'Be taken up and cast into the sea,' it shall happen" (Matthew 21:21).

In Mark 11:23 Jesus speaks not merely to the disciples then present, "If you have faith . . . " but by the word "whoever" He extends His promise to all believers: "Truly I say to you, whoever says to this mountain, 'Be taken up and cast into the sea,' and does not doubt in his heart, but believes that what he says is going to happen; it shall be granted him." Jesus sets no limit to the scope of this kind of faith. The phrases He uses are all-inclusive: "Whoever says . . . what he says . . . shall be granted him." There is no restriction as to the person who speaks or the words that are spoken. All that matters is the nature of the faith: it must be God's own faith.

In Luke 8:22–25 we have the story of Jesus and His disciples crossing the Sea of Galilee in a boat, suddenly overtaken by an unnaturally violent storm. The disciples awoke Jesus, who was asleep in the stern, saying, "Master, Master, we are perishing!" The record continues, "And being aroused, He rebuked the wind and the surging waves, and they stopped, and it became calm."

Obviously the faith that Jesus exercised here was not on the human level. Normally the winds and the waters are not under man's control. But at the moment of need Jesus received a special impartation of God's own faith. Then, by a word spoken with that faith, He accomplished what otherwise only God alone could have done—the instantaneous calming of the storm.

When the danger had passed, Jesus turned to His disciples and said, "Where is *your* faith?" In other words, He asked "Why couldn't *you* have done that? Why did *I* have to do it?" He implied that it would have been just as easy for the disciples to calm the storm as it was for Him—if they had exercised the right kind of faith. But in the moment of crisis the impact of the storm on the disciples' senses had opened the way for fear to enter their hearts, thus excluding faith. Jesus, on the other hand, had opened His heart to the Father and received from Him the supernatural gift of faith needed to deal with the storm.

Quality, Not Quantity

Later, Jesus confronted a storm of a different kind—a boy rolling on the ground in an epileptic seizure and an agonized father imploring help. Jesus dealt with this storm as He had dealt with the one on the Sea of Galilee. He spoke an authoritative word of faith that drove the evil spirit out of the boy. When His disciples asked Him why they had not been able to do this, He told them plainly, "Because of the littleness of your faith." Then He went on to say, "If you have faith as a mustard seed, you shall say to this mountain, 'Move from here to there,' and it shall move; and nothing shall be impossible to you" (Matthew 17:20).

Jesus here uses a mustard seed as a measure of quantity. In Matthew 13:32 we are told that a mustard seed is "smaller than all other seeds." In other words, Jesus is telling us, it is not the *quantity* of the faith that matters, but the *quality*. A mustard seed of this kind of faith is sufficient to move a mountain!

Near the climax of His earthly ministry, outside the tomb of Lazarus, Jesus once more demonstrated the power of words spoken with this kind of faith. He cried out with a loud voice, "Lazarus, come forth" (John 11:43). This brief command, energized by supernatural faith, caused a man who was both dead and buried to come walking out of his tomb, alive and well.

The original pattern for this kind of faith is found in the act of creation itself. It was by faith in His own word that God brought the universe into being. "By the word of the LORD the heavens were made, And by the breath [literally, spirit] of His mouth all their host . . . For He spoke, and it was done; He commanded, and it stood fast" (Psalm 33:6,9). God's spoken word, energized by His Spirit, was the effective agent in all creation.

When the gift of faith is in operation, a man becomes, for a time, the channel of God's own faith. The *person* who speaks is no longer important, but only the *faith* that is expressed. If it is God's own faith at work, it is equally effective whether the words are spoken through God's mouth or whether they are uttered by the Holy Spirit through the mouth of a human believer. So long as a believer operates with this divine faith, his words are just as effective as if God Himself had spoken them. It is the *faith* that matters, not the person.

In the examples which we have considered hitherto, this supernatural faith was expressed through a spoken word. It was by a spoken word that Jesus caused the fig tree to wither. By a spoken word, too, he calmed the storm, cast the evil spirit out of the epileptic boy and called Lazarus out of the tomb. In Mark 11:23 He extended this promise to any word spoken in faith when He said, "Whoever says . . . what he says . . . shall be granted him."

Sometimes a word spoken in prayer becomes the channel for the gift of faith. In James 5:15 we are told that "the *prayer of faith** will restore the one who is sick." There is no room left for doubt as to the effect of such a prayer as is described here. Its results are guaranteed. Prayer prayed with this kind of God-given

* This is the literal translation given in the margin.

faith is irresistible. Neither sickness nor any other condition that is contrary to God's will can stand against it.

As an example of "the prayer of faith," James refers to Elijah, who by his prayer first withheld all rain for three-and-a-half years, and then caused rain to fall again (James 5:17–18). The Scripture indicates that the giving and withholding of rain is a divine prerogative, exercised by God Himself (see, for example, Deuteronomy 11:13–17; Jeremiah 5:24; 14:22). Yet for three-and-a-half years Elijah exercised this prerogative on God's behalf. James emphasizes that Elijah was "a man with a nature like ours"—a human being just like the rest of us. But so long as he was enabled to pray with God's faith, the words he uttered were as effective as God's own decrees.

However, faith of this kind need not operate only through a spoken word. It was by the same kind of supernatural faith that Jesus was able to walk on the stormy Sea of Galilee (see Matthew 14:25–33). In this case, He did not need to speak; He merely walked out over the water. Peter began to follow the example of Jesus and to exercise the same kind of faith. This enabled him to do just the same as Jesus was doing. But when he looked away from Jesus to the waves, his faith deserted him and he began to sink!

The comment that Jesus made is very illuminating. "O you of little faith, why did you doubt?" (Matthew 14:31). Jesus did not reprove Peter for wanting to walk on the water. He reproved him for losing faith halfway. Don Basham has pointed out that there is a divine urge, implanted in every human heart, to step out in supernatural faith and walk on a plane above the level of our own ability. Since God Himself placed this urge in man, He does not reprove us for it. On the contrary, He is willing to give us the faith that will enable us to do it. He is disappointed, not when we reach out for this kind of faith, but only when we do not hold on to it long enough.

God Retains the Initiative

This supernatural kind of faith is given in a specific situation to meet a specific need. It remains under God's direct control. It must remain so, for it is God's own faith. He gives it or withholds it at His discretion. It is included with all the other supernatural gifts, concerning which Paul says, "But one and the same Spirit works all these things, distributing to each one individually just as He wills" (1 Corinthians 12:11). The key phrase here is at the end—"just as *He* wills." God Himself determines when and to whom He will impart each of these gifts. The initiative is with God, not with man.

This was true even in the ministry of Jesus Himself. He did not curse every fruitless fig tree; He did not still every tempest; He did not call every dead man out of his tomb; He did not always walk on the water. He was careful to leave the initiative in the hands of His Father. In John 5:19 He said, "The Son can do nothing of Himself, unless it is something He sees the Father doing; for whatever the Father does, these things the Son also does in like manner." Again, in John 14:10, "The words that I say to you I do not speak on My own initiative, but the Father abiding in me does His works." Always the initiative was with the Father.

We must learn to be as reverent and as careful in our relationship to the Father as Jesus was. The gift of faith is not ours to command. It is not intended to satisfy our personal whims or ambitions. It is made available at God's discretion to accomplish ends which originate in

God's own eternal purposes. We cannot, and must not, wrest the initiative from God. Even if God should permit us to do so, it would ultimately be to our own loss.

Pictured as a "mustard seed," the gift of faith is similar to two of the gifts of revelation—the word of wisdom and the word of knowledge. Wisdom is directive; knowledge is informative. God has all wisdom and all knowledge, but, fortunately for us, He does not burden us with all of it. However, in a given situation where we need direction, He supernaturally imparts to us a "word" of wisdom—just one little "mustard seed" out of His total store of wisdom. Or in a situation where we need information, He imparts to us a "word" of knowledge—a little "mustard seed" out of His total store of knowledge.

So it is with the gift of faith. God has all faith, but He does not impart it all to us. In a given situation, where we need faith on a higher level than our own, God imparts to us a "mustard seed" out of His own total store. Once this special need has been met, God withdraws *His* faith and we are left once again to exercise our own.

Equipment for Evangelism

From another point of view, as we have seen earlier, the gift of faith is associated with the other two gifts of power: the gifts of healing and the effecting of miracles. In practice, the gift of faith often serves as a catalyst to bring the other two gifts into operation. This is exemplified by the ministry of Philip in Samaria, as described in Acts 8:5–8:

(5)   And Philip went down to the city of Samaria

and began proclaiming Christ to them.

(6) And the multitudes with one accord were giving attention to what was said by Philip, as they heard and saw the signs which he was performing.

(7) For in the case of many who had unclean spirits, they were coming out of them shouting with a loud voice; and many who had been paralyzed and lame were healed.

(8) And there was much rejoicing in that city.

In the first phase of his ministry, Philip cast out evil spirits. As we have seen from the example of Jesus—in Matthew 17:17–20 and elsewhere—this was done by the spoken word through the exercise of the gift of faith. In the second phase of Philip's ministry the two associated gifts of *healings* and *miracles* came into operation. As a result, miracles were performed and the paralyzed and the lame were healed.

In Acts 21:8 Philip is called "the evangelist." There are only two actual patterns of the ministry of the evangelist presented to us in the New Testament: that of Jesus Himself and that of Philip. In each case, there was a strong emphasis on casting out evil spirits, followed by miracles and healings. The three gifts of faith, miracles, and healings together constitute the supernatural equipment, endorsed by the New Testament, for the ministry of the evangelist.

Summary

The gift of faith is one of nine gifts of the Holy Spirit listed by Paul in 1 Corinthians 12:7–11. Each of these gifts is a supernatural manifestation of the Holy Spirit, dwelling in a believer and operating through him.

Through the gift of faith, the Holy Spirit temporarily imparts to a believer a portion of God's own faith. This is faith on a divine level, far above the human. It is not the quantity that matters, but the quality. A "mustard seed" of this kind of faith is sufficient to move a mountain.

The gift of faith operates frequently, but not exclusively, through a spoken word. Such a word may be spoken in prayer. Through this gift Jesus caused a fig tree to wither in 24 hours, calmed a storm at sea, drove an evil spirit out of an epileptic boy, called Lazarus out of his tomb, and walked on the stormy waves.

God has implanted in man an urge to exercise this kind of faith. Therefore He does not reprove us for doing so. Rather, He is disappointed if we let go of it too soon. However, as in the ministry of Jesus, the initiative must always be left with God.

The gift of faith can serve as a catalyst for the related gifts of healing and miracles. These three gifts combined are the equipment endorsed by the New Testament for the ministry of an evangelist.

Chapter Four

Faith as a Fruit

In the preceding chapter we looked at the nine spiritual gifts listed by Paul in 1 Corinthians 12:8–10. In this chapter we will turn to the list of the nine forms of spiritual fruit which Paul gives in Galatians 5:22–23: "But the fruit of the Spirit is love, joy, peace, longsuffering, gentleness, goodness, faith, meekness, temperance . . ." (KJV).

The seventh form of fruit here listed is *faith.* Recent versions offer a variety of translations, such as: "faithfulness," "fidelity," "trustfulness." However, the Greek noun which Paul here uses is *pistis.* As we saw in chapter 1, this is the basic word for "faith" throughout the New Testament.

Before we begin to study this particular form of fruit, it will be helpful first to consider the relationship between gifts and fruit in general. What is the difference between them?

Fruit vs. Gifts

One way to bring the difference into focus is to

picture a Christmas tree and an apple tree side by side. A Christmas tree bears gifts; an apple tree bears fruit. A gift is both attached to a Christmas tree and removed from it by a single, brief act. The gift may be a garment and the tree may be a fir tree. There is no direct connection between the tree and the gift. The gift tells us nothing about the nature of the tree from which it is taken.

On the other hand, there is a direct connection between an apple and the tree which bears it. The nature of the tree determines the nature of the fruit, both as to kind and as to quality. An apple tree can never bear an orange. A healthy tree will bear healthy fruit; an unhealthy tree will bear unhealthy fruit (see Matthew 7:17–20). The fruit on the apple tree is not produced by a single act, but is the result of a steady, continuing process of growth and development. To produce the best fruit, the tree must be carefully cultivated. This requires time, skill, and labor.

Let us apply this simple analogy to the spiritual realm. A spiritual gift is both imparted and received by a single, brief transaction. It tells us nothing about the nature of the person who exercises it. On the other hand, spiritual fruit expresses the nature of the life from which it proceeds; it comes only as the result of a process of growth. To attain the best fruit, a life must be carefully cultivated—with time, skill, and labor.

We may express the difference in another way by saying that gifts express *ability,* fruit expresses *character.*

Which is more important? In the long run, undoubtedly, character is more important than ability. The exercise of gifts is temporary. As Paul explains in 1 Corinthians 13:8–13, there will come a time when gifts will no longer be needed. But character is permanent.

The character we develop in this life will determine what we will be throughout eternity. We will one day leave our gifts behind; our character will be with us forever.

However, we do not need to choose one at the expense of the other. Gifts do not exclude fruit; fruit does not exclude gifts. Rather, they are intended to complement each other. Gifts should provide practical expression for character. This is perfectly exemplified in the person of Jesus Himself. His loving, gracious character was expressed by the fullest possible exercise of spiritual gifts. Only through these could He meet the needs of the people to whom He had come to minister and thus fully express to them the nature of His heavenly Father whom he had come to represent (see John 14:9–10).

We should seek to follow His pattern. The more we develop the attributes of love, concern, and compassion that characterized Jesus, the more we will need the same gifts that He exercised in order to give practical expression to these attributes. The more fully we are equipped with these gifts, the greater will be our ability to glorify God our Father, just as Jesus did.

Faith as Trust

Fruit then, expresses character. When all nine forms of spiritual fruit are present and fully developed, they represent the totality of Christian character, perfectly rounded off, each form of fruit satisfying a specific need and each complementing the rest. Within this totality, the fruit of faith may be viewed from two aspects, corresponding to two different, but related, uses of the Greek word *pistis.* The first is *trust;* the second is *trustworthiness.*

To express the first aspect of faith as a fruit, the Jerusalem Bible translates *pistis* as "trustfulness." Many times over, Jesus emphasized that one essential requirement for all who would enter the Kingdom of God is to become as little children (see Matthew 8:1–4; 19:13–14; Mark 10:13–15; Luke 18:16–17). Probably there is no quality more distinctively characteristic of childhood than *trustfulness.* And yet, by a paradox, it is a quality that is seen at its perfection in the most mature men of God—men such as Abraham, Moses, David, or Paul. We may conclude, therefore, that the degree to which we cultivate this particular form of fruit provides a good measure of our spiritual maturity.

More fully, the fruit of faith—in this aspect—may be defined as a quiet, steady, unwavering trust in the goodness, wisdom, and faithfulness of God. No matter what trials or seeming disasters may be encountered, the person who has cultivated this form of fruit remains calm and restful in the midst of it all. He has an unshakable confidence that God is still in complete control of every situation and that, in and through all circumstances, God is working out His own purposes of blessing for each one of His children.

The outward expression of this kind of trust is *stability.* This is beautifully pictured by David in Psalm 125:1: "Those who trust in the LORD are as Mount Zion, which cannot be moved, but abides for ever." All earth's mountains may tremble and shake and even be totally removed—except one. Zion is the mountain which God has chosen for His own dwelling place. It alone can never be moved, but abides forever.

So it is with the believer who has learned to trust. Others all around may give way to panic and confusion, but he remains calm and secure. "His foundation is in the holy mountains" (Psalm 87:1).

About 1960, while I was serving as principal of a training college for African teachers in western Kenya, one of our women students, named Agneta, contracted typhoid. My wife and I visited her in the hospital and found her critically ill, in a deep coma. I prayed that God would bring her out of the coma long enough for me to speak to her. A moment later, she opened her eyes and looked up at me.

"Agneta," I said, "do you know for sure that your soul is safe in the Lord's hands?"

"Yes," she said in a clear, firm voice—and immediately lapsed into a coma again. But I was satisfied. That one word "Yes" was all she needed to say and all I needed to hear. It expressed a deep, untroubled trust which nothing in this world could shake or overthrow.

The key to this kind of trust is *commitment.* About a year previously, in my presence, Agneta made a definite, personal commitment of her life to Jesus Christ. Now in the hour of testing—perhaps at the very threshhold of eternity—she did not need to make any further commitment. She needed only to rest in the commitment she had already made—one which included both life and death, both time and eternity.

In due course, God answered the prayers of Agneta's fellow students and raised her up again to full health. Her ability to "receive" the influence of the prayers offered on her behalf was in large measure due to her attitude of trust.

In Psalm 37:5 David says, "Commit your way to the LORD, trust also in Him, and He will do it." More literally the verse says, "and He is doing it." Two things are here required of us. The first is an act, "commit." The second is an attitude, "trust." The *act* of commitment leads to the *attitude* of trust. So long as we continue in this attitude of trust, David assures us, God "is doing it." In other words, God is working out the thing that we have committed to Him. It is the continuing attitude of trust on our part that keeps open the channel through which God is able to intervene in our life and work out what needs to be done. But if we abandon our trust, we close off the channel and hinder the completion of what God has begun to do for us.

Committing a matter to the Lord is like taking cash to the bank and depositing it in our account. Once we have received the teller's receipt for our deposit, we need no longer be concerned about the safety of our money. That is now the bank's responsibility, not ours. It is somewhat ironical that people who have no difficulty in trusting a bank to take care of the money they have deposited find it much harder to trust God concerning some vital, personal matter which they have committed to Him.

The example of the bank deposit illustrates one important factor in making a successful commitment. When we walk out of the bank, we carry an official receipt, indicating the date, the place, and the amount of our deposit. There are no uncertainties. We need to be equally specific concerning those things that we commit to God. We need to know, without a shadow of doubt, both *what* we have committed and *when* and *where* the commitment was made. We also need the Holy Spirit's official "receipt," acknowledging that God has accepted our commitment.

Trust Must Be Cultivated

Trust is like all forms of fruit: it needs to be cultivated and it passes through various stages of development before it reaches full maturity. The development of trust is well illustrated by the words of David in Psalm 62. In verse 2 he says, "He [God] only is my rock and my salvation, my stronghold; I shall not be *greatly shaken*." But in verse 6, after making exactly the same declaration of trust in God, he says, "I shall not be *shaken*." Between verse 2 and verse 6, David has progressed from not being "greatly shaken" to not being "shaken" at all.*

We need to be as honest about ourselves as David was. Before our trust has come to maturity, the best that we can say is, "I shall not be greatly shaken!" At this stage, troubles and opposition will shake us, but they will not overthrow us. However, if we continue to cultivate our trust, we shall come to the stage where we can say, "I shall not be shaken"—period! Nothing will any longer be able even to shake us—much less overthrow us.

Trust of this kind is in the realm of the spirit, rather than the emotions. We may turn once more to the personal testimony of David for an illustration. In Psalm 56:3 he says to the Lord, "When I am afraid, I will put my trust in Thee." Here David recognizes two conflicting influences at work in himself simultaneously: trust and fear. But fear is superficial, in the emotions; trust is deeper down, in the spirit.

Mature trust is like a deep, strong river, making its irresistible way to the sea. At times, the winds of fear or doubt may blow contrary to the river's course and whip up foaming waves on its surface. But these winds and waves cannot change or hinder the deep, continuing flow of the waters below the surface, as they follow the path marked out for them by the river's bed to their predetermined end in the sea.

Trust in its full maturity is beautifully exemplified by the words of Paul in 2 Timothy 1:12: "For this reason I also suffer these things, but I am not ashamed; for I

*In chapter 7 we will deal more fully with the need to "confess" our faith by verbal affirmation and reaffirmation.

know whom I have believed and I am convinced that He is able to guard what I have entrusted to Him until that day." By all worldly standards, Paul at this stage was a failure. Some of his most influential friends and supporters had turned against him. Of all his close co-workers, only Luke remained with him; one of them, Demas, had actually abandoned him and turned back to the world. Paul was infirm and aged, a manacled prisoner in a Roman jail, awaiting unjust trial and execution at the hands of a cruel, depraved despot. Yet his words ring with serene, unshakable confidence: "I am not ashamed . . . I know . . . I have believed . . . I am convinced . . . ." Beyond the horizon of time he looks forward to an unclouded day—"that day"—the day when another, righteous Judge will award him "the crown of righteousness" (see 2 Timothy 4:8).

For Paul as for David, trust was the outcome of an act of *commitment.* It is expressed in his own words: "He is able to guard what *I have entrusted* to Him . . . ." "Trusting" was the result of "entrusting." Years previously Paul had made an irrevocable commitment of himself to Christ. Out of this, subsequent trials and sufferings gradually brought forth an ever-deepening trust that had now come to its full fruition in a Roman dungeon, its radiance all the brighter by contrast with its gloomy setting.

Faith as Trustworthiness

We turn now to the second aspect of faith as a fruit: *trustworthiness.* Linguistically, trustworthiness is in fact the original meaning of *pistis.* In Arndt and Gingrich's standard lexicon of New Testament Greek, the first specific definition given of *pistis* is: "faithfulness, reliability." If we go back to the Old Testament, the same applies to the Hebrew word for faith—*emunah*. Its primary meaning is "faithfulness"; its secondary meaning is "faith." The verb from which it is derived gives us the word *Amen*—"So be it," "Let it be confirmed." The root thought is "firm, reliable."

Both meanings alike—trust and trustworthiness—converge in the person and nature of God Himself. If we view faith as *trust*, its only ultimate basis is God's *trustworthiness*. If we view faith as *trustworthiness*, it is only through our *trust* that the Holy Spirit is able to impart to us God's *trustworthiness*. God Himself is both the beginning and the end of faith. His *trustworthiness* is the only basis for our *trust*; our *trust* in Him reproduces in us His *trustworthiness*.

Probably no attribute of God is more persistently emphasized throughout the Scriptures than His trustworthiness. In the Old Testament there is one special Hebrew word reserved for this attribute: *chesed*. In the English versions this word is variously translated "goodness," "kindness," "lovingkindness," "mercy," etc. However, none of these translations fully expresses its meaning.

There are two distinctive features of God's *chesed*. First, it is the expression of God's free, unmerited *grace*. It goes beyond anything that man can ever deserve or demand as a right. Second, it is always based on a *covenant* that God voluntarily enters into. We may combine these two features by saying that *chesed* is God's trustworthiness in fulfilling His covenant commitments, which go beyond anything that we can deserve or demand.

We thus find a close connection between three important Hebrew concepts: *emunah*, faith or faithfulness; *chesed*, God's trustworthiness; *berith*, a covenant. This is the recurrent theme of a series of verses in Psalm 89:

(24)   And My faithfulness *(emunah)* and My lovingkindness *(chesed)* will be with him . . .

(28)   My lovingkindness *(chesed)* I will keep for him forever,
And My covenant *(berith)* shall be confirmed *(amen)* to him.

(33)   But I will not break off My lovingkindness *(chesed)* from him,
Nor deal falsely in My faithfulness *(emunah)*.

(34)   My covenant *(berith)* I will not violate,
Nor will I alter the utterance of my lips.

This last verse brings out a special relationship between God's trustworthiness and the words of His mouth. There are two things God will never do: break His covenant, or go back on what He has said. God's trustworthiness, imparted by the Holy Spirit, will reproduce the same characteristics in us. It will make us persons of unfailing integrity and honesty.

In Psalm 15:1 David asks two questions: "LORD, who may abide in Thy tent? Who may dwell on Thy holy hill?" In the following verses he answers his own questions by listing 11 characteristics that mark a person of this kind. The ninth requirement, listed at the end of verse 4, is, "He swears to his own hurt, and does not change." God expects the believer to be true to his commitments, even at the cost of personal sacrifice. The world has its own way of saying this: "A man is as good as his word." A Christian who does not honor his word and keep his commitments has not yet developed the fruit of trustworthiness.

While God requires this kind of trustworthiness in our dealings with all men, we have a special obligation toward our fellow Christians. God's own trustworthiness *(chesed)* is based, as we have seen, upon His covenant *(berith).* Through Jesus Christ He has brought us into a covenant relationship both with Himself and with one another. The distinguishing mark of this relationship is that we exhibit, both toward God and toward our fellow believers, the same trustworthiness that God has so richly and freely demonstrated toward us.

We have already seen that God's *chesed,* expressed in His covenant commitments, is based on His *grace,* going beyond anything that we, who are its recipients, can ever deserve or demand. This too will be reflected in our covenant relationships with our fellow believers. We will not limit ourselves to the mere requirements of justice or of some legal form of contract. We will be ready to make the full commitment that God made in establishing His covenant with us—to lay down our lives for one another. "We know love by this, that He laid down His life for us; and we ought to lay down our lives for the brethren" (1 John 3:16). It is by the laying down of our lives that we enter into full covenant relationship with God and with one another.

Scripture paints a fearful picture of the breakdown of moral and ethical standards that will mark the close of this present age:

> You must face the fact: the final age of this world is to be a time of troubles. Men will love nothing but money and self; they will be arrogant, boastful, and abusive; with no respect for parents, no gratitude, no piety, no natural affection; they will be implacable in their hatreds, scandal-mongers, intemperate and fierce, strangers to all goodness,

traitors, adventurers, swollen with self-importance. They will be men who put pleasure in the place of God, men who preserve the outward form of religion, but are a standing denial of its reality. Keep clear of men like these (2 Timothy 3:1–4, NEB).

The Greek word translated above "implacable in their hatreds" is defined in Thayer's lexicon as denoting "those who cannot be persuaded to enter into a covenant." The whole trend of this world will be—indeed, already is—away from those moral and ethical characteristics which covenant demands. As the world thus plunges deeper into darkness, God's people must—by contrast—be more determined than ever to walk in the light of fellowship. We must show ourselves both willing and qualified to enter into and maintain those covenant relationships upon which fellowship depends.

For this purpose we will need to cultivate to full maturity the fruit of trustworthiness.

Summary

Spiritual fruit differs from spiritual gifts in two main ways. First, a spiritual gift can be both imparted and received by a single, brief transaction; fruit must be cultivated by a continuing process, requiring time, skill, and labor. Second, gifts are not directly related to the character of those who exercise them; fruit is an expression of character. Ideally, fruit and gifts should balance one another in a combination that glorifies God and serves humanity.

As a form of fruit, faith may be understood in two

distinct but related ways: as trust and as trustworthiness.

Trust is manifested in stability, which increases as trust matures. It requires an initial act of commitment. "Entrusting" leads to "trusting."

Our trust is based on God's trustworthiness (Hebrew *chesed*). God demonstrates His trustworthiness toward us by fulfilling His covenant commitments, which go beyond anything we can deserve or demand. In turn, it makes us the kind of people who are willing and able to enter into and maintain covenant commitments, both with God and with one another.

Chapter Five

Faith to Live By

About six centuries before the Christian era, God gave the prophet Habakkuk a revelation that was to provide the basis of the gospel: "But the righteous will live by his faith" (Habakkuk 2:4). So accurately does this prophecy express the central theme of the Christian message that it is actually quoted three times in the New Testament: in Romans 1:17; in Galatians 3:11; and in Hebrews 10:38.

Only One Basis: Faith

Of these three passages, Habakkuk's prophecy is most fully expounded in Romans. In fact, it provides the central theme for the whole epistle. To obtain a proper perspective on Romans as a whole, we may compare it to a symphony by a great composer such as Beethoven. The first 15 verses of chapter 1 are the introduction. Then in verses 16 and 17 Paul presents the main theme: "BUT THE RIGHTEOUS *MAN* SHALL LIVE BY FAITH."

The symphony is then divided into three main

movements. The first consists of chapters 1 through 8. In this movement Paul's approach is *doctrinal.* He works out a detailed, logical analysis of his theme, showing how it harmonizes with the prophecies and the patterns of the Old Testament. The second movement consists of chapters 9, 10 and 11. Here Paul applies his theme to *Israel.* He shows how Israel's attempt to achieve righteousness by works rather than by faith blinded them to their Messiah and so deprived them of the blessings offered to them by God through Him. The third movement consists of chapters 12 through 16. Here Paul's emphasis is *practical.* He shows how his theme must be worked out in various activities, relationships, and duties of daily living.

To appreciate a symphony properly, we need to pick out the composer's main theme when it is first introduced and then follow it carefully through the whole piece. Unless we keep the main theme in mind, we will not fully appreciate the various modifications and developments it undergoes in the successive movements. The same principle applies to Romans. First of all, we need to grasp the main theme which runs throughout the whole epistle: "The righteous man will live by faith." Then we need to keep this theme always in mind as we study the epistle's main divisions, noting how it applies to each particular subject that is dealt with. This will give unity and consistency to our understanding of the whole epistle.

In Romans 1:16 Paul states the one basic requirement for experiencing the power of God for salvation:

> For I am not ashamed of the gospel, for it is the power of God for salvation to every one who believes, to the Jew first and also to the Greek.

Salvation is here made available to *"every one who believes*—to the Jew first and also to the Greek." There are no exceptions. Differences of religious or racial background are irrelevant. In God's all-inclusive offer of salvation to the human race, He has laid down one simple requirement that never varies. It is *faith.*

In verse 17 Paul goes on to explain how this truth of salvation can be known.

> For in it [the gospel] the righteousness of God is revealed from faith to faith; as it is written, "BUT THE RIGHTEOUS *MAN* SHALL LIVE BY FAITH."

The word "faith" occurs three times in this verse. God's revelation comes *from* faith *to* faith. It originates in God's own faith—faith that His word will accomplish its preordained purpose. It is transmitted through the faith of the one who delivers the message. It is appropriated by the faith of the one who receives the message. And the message itself is, "The righteous man will live by faith." From beginning to end, the theme is *faith.*

Let us examine the message more closely. It could not be more simply stated: "The righteous man will live by faith." Obviously to "live," in this context, means more than to have normal, physical life. We know that even the wicked and the ungodly have that kind of life. But Scripture reveals that there is another kind of life—a life of righteousness—that has its source in God alone. The only way that anyone can receive this kind of life is *by faith in Jesus Christ.*

In his Gospel the apostle John continually dwells on this divine, eternal life. At the opening, in John 1:4, he tells us concerning Jesus, "In Him was life." In John 3:36 he records the testimony of John the Baptist concerning Jesus: "He who believes in the Son has eternal life." In John 6:47 Jesus Himself says, "He who believes has eternal life." Again, in John 10:10, "I came that they might have life, and might have it abundantly." And in John 10:27–28: "My sheep hear My voice, and I know them, and they follow Me; and I give eternal life to them." Finally, at the close of his Gospel, John states the main purpose for which it was written: "that you may believe that Jesus is the Christ, the Son of God; and that believing you may have life in His name" (John 20:31).

In chapter 5 of his First Epistle, John returns to this theme:

(11) And the witness is this, that God has given us eternal life, and this life is in His Son.

(12) He who has the Son has the life; he who does not have the Son of God does not have the life.

(13) These things I have written to you who believe in the name of the Son of God, in order that you may know that you have eternal life.

It is important to see that John uses the present tense throughout. "He who has the Son *has* the life." "You who believe" *already* "*have* eternal life."

Paul also speaks of this life in Christ in brief and vivid phrases. In Philippians 1:21 he says, "For to me, to live is Christ." And in Colossians 3:4, "Christ . . . is our life." For Paul, as for John, this is a present reality, not just a future hope.

This, then, is the essence of the gospel message. There is a divine, eternal life which has its source in God alone. God has made this life available to us in Jesus Christ. As we receive Jesus by faith in our hearts and yield our lives to Him in full obedience, we receive in Him the very life of God Himself. This life is not something reserved for another world or a future existence. It is something that we can experience here and now. "He who has the Son has the life." He has it at this very moment—and on into eternity. Eternal life is ours to enjoy from the very moment that we truly put our faith in Jesus Christ.

Having thus received this new kind of life through faith in Christ, we are faced with the challenge of working it out from day to day in practical living. How are we to do this? The answer is simple: *by faith.* This too is contained in Paul's opening theme: "The righteous man will live by faith." Viewed from the practical standpoint, the verb "to live" is one of the most all-inclusive words we can use. Everything we do at any time is included in *living:* eating, drinking, sleeping, working, and innumerable other activities necessary to life. Through faith, every one of these commonplace activities can become a way to express the life of God that we have received within us.

We are often prone to assume that the mundane actions of daily life have no spiritual significance and offer no place for the application of our faith. But actually Scripture teaches the opposite. It is only after we have successfully applied our faith in the simple, material areas of life that God will promote us to higher spiritual responsibilities. Jesus Himself lays down this principle in Luke 16:10–11:

(10)   "He who is faithful in a very little thing is faithful also in much; and he who is unrighteous in a very little thing is unrighteous also in much.

(11)   "If therefore you have not been faithful in the use of unrighteous Mammon [money], who will entrust the true riches to you?"

Only after we have made our faith work in the "very little things" and in the area of money will God entrust to us the greater responsibilities and the true spiritual riches.

Therefore, in examining how we can work out our faith in daily living, we will consider two practical, down-to-earth areas: food and finance. From many years of personal observation I have concluded that a believer who has learned to apply his faith in these two is likely to be leading a successful Christian life. On the other hand, if a person has not brought these basic areas under God's control, it is usually an indication that his whole life needs to be adjusted.

Eating from Faith

We have stated already that the "third movement" of the Romans "symphony" focuses on the practical application of our faith and opens at the beginning of chapter 12. What does it start with? Something remote or ethereal? No! On the contrary, it begins—in the very first verse—with *our bodies:*

> I urge you therefore, brethren, by the mercies of God, to present *your bodies* a living and holy sacrifice, acceptable to God, which is your spiritual service of worship (Romans 12:1).

Paul tells us that our "spiritual service of worship" consists in presenting our bodies to God. In other words, to be "spiritual" is to be very practical and down-to-earth. It starts with what we do with our bodies!*

From this starting point Paul goes on to deal with a

---

*In chapter 10 we will examine in detail the results that follow from thus "presenting our bodies to God."

variety of practical issues related to the Christian life. In chapter 14 he deals with the issue of food. (Obviously there is no issue of greater importance to our physical body than this!) He considers two types of believer: "One man has faith that he may eat all things, but he who is weak eats vegetables only" (Romans 14:2). Paul does not settle this issue by saying, absolutely, that it is right to eat vegetables and wrong to eat meat, or vice versa. Rather he says that anything we can do in faith is right, and anything we cannot do in faith is wrong. He states his conclusion in the closing verse of the chapter: "But he who doubts is condemned if he eats, because his eating is not from faith; and *whatever is not from faith is sin*" (Romans 14:23).

By his closing statement Paul goes beyond the mere issue of eating meat or vegetables and reaffirms the principle that was his opening theme at the beginning of the epistle. In Romans 1:17 he stated it positively: "The righteous man shall live by faith." Here in Romans 14:23 he states the same principle negatively: "Whatever is not from faith is sin." Viewed positively or negatively, the conclusion is the same: *faith is the only basis for righteous living.*

Let us then accept this challenge of applying our faith to our eating. We are required to "eat from faith." This is a rather strange phrase. How can we apply it in a practical way?

Several things are involved. First of all, it means that we acknowledge our dependence upon God for our food. We receive it as a gift from Him. If He did not supply it, we would go hungry.

Secondly, as a logical consequence, we thank God for our food.

Thanking God for our food in turn produces a third consequence, explained by Paul in 1 Timothy 4:4–5:

(4) For everything created by God is good, and nothing is to be rejected, if it is received with gratitude [literally, thanksgiving]:

(5) for it is sanctified by means of the word of God and prayer.

As we receive our food from God with a prayer of thanksgiving, it is "sanctified": it actually becomes something holy, designed by God to do us good. Even if there were originally impure or harmful ingredients in our food, their effect is nullified by our faith, expressed in our prayer of thanksgiving.

Fourthly, "eating from faith" has implications that go beyond the meal table. Our food is the source of our natural strength, and God is the source of our food. Therefore our strength is itself a gift from God. We are not free to use it in selfish or sinful ways, but we are under an obligation to devote it to God's service and God's glory.

As we thus apply the principle of faith to our eating, this whole area of our lives gains a new significance. We can understand how Paul could exhort the believers at Corinth, "Whether, then, you eat or drink or whatever you do, do all to the glory of God" (1 Corinthians 10:31). Through faith, even our daily meals take on the nature of a sacrament, of which we partake for God's glory. This was one of the most immediate and obvious effects produced in the lives of the first Christians by the outpouring of the Holy Spirit on the day of Pentecost. Their meals became spiritual feasts of worship and praise. In Acts 2:46—47 Luke records:

(46) And day by day continuing with one mind in the temple, and breaking bread from house to house, they were taking their

> meals together with gladness and sincerity of heart,
>
> (47) praising God, and having favor with all the people. And the Lord was adding to their number day by day those who were being saved.

There was something so different about the way these Christians actually ate their meals that it gained them the favor of their unconverted neighbors and won them to the Lord. It can be the same with us today when we put our faith to work in this area of eating!

If the consequences of "eating from faith" are so far-reaching, what about the consequences of failing to eat in this way? For a vivid picture of the man who does *not* eat from faith we may turn to the book of Ecclesiastes. (Few Christians spend much time in Ecclesiastes, but—when interpreted in the light of other, more familiar scriptures—it contains some real treasures.) Throughout most of the book, Solomon is describing what the Bible elsewhere calls the "natural man"—that is, the man who, through unbelief, lives his life without the grace and the knowledge of God. In Ecclesiastes 5:17 Solomon pictures such a man at his meal table: "Throughout his life he also eats in darkness with great vexation, sickness and anger."

What striking language! "He eats in darkness." What does it mean? It means just the opposite of "eating from faith." Such a man does not acknowledge his food as a gift from God. He does not thank God for it. Therefore it is not blessed and sanctified. What is the result? "Great vexation, sickness and anger." To eat without faith is to invite vexation, sickness and anger.

We have examined rather carefully how the principle of faith applies to one of our most common daily activities—eating. As a result, we are now in a position to understand more fully the scope of Romans 1:17—"the righteous man will live by faith." Faith, we can now see, is the channel of divine life. The more faith we exercise, the more life we enjoy. Every activity to which we apply our faith becomes permeated with divine life. It is no longer drab or commonplace. It becomes fresh, exciting, joyous—an occasion for worship and praise!

Faith for Finance

Another area of everyday living in which we need to apply the principle of faith is that of financial and material provision. The whole Bible abounds with both assurances and examples of God's ability to provide for His people's needs—even in situations where there is no human or natural source of supply. Nowhere is this more emphatically stated than in 2 Corinthians 9:8: "And God is able to make *all* grace *abound* to you, that *always* having *all* sufficiency in *everything,* you may have an *abundance* for *every* good deed." It is worthwhile to examine this verse closely. Where the English translation uses the word "every," the Greek uses "all." Thus in the original text the word "abound"—or "abundance"—occurs twice and the word "all" occurs five times. It is hard to see how language could express more forcefully the ability of God to provide for every area of His people's needs. The level of provision it reveals is not mere sufficiency; it is *abundance.*

There are actually three levels of provision on which people may live: insufficiency; sufficiency; and abundance. We may illustrate these from the simple, everyday example of a housewife shopping for groceries. A housewife who needs $15 worth of groceries and has

$10 in her purse is shopping out of *insufficiency*. A housewife who needs $15 worth of groceries and has $15 in her purse is shopping out of *sufficiency*. But a housewife who needs $15 worth of groceries and has $20 is shopping out of *abundance*.

In this rather simple example, we have pictured a housewife buying groceries with dollars. However, it must be emphasized that "abundance" does not necessarily depend on money or material possessions. Abundance means simply that God supplies all that we need—with something to spare for others. The perfect example of this form of abundance is provided by Jesus Himself. He had no fixed dwelling, no material possessions, no large sums of money—although Judas, one of His disciples, did carry a money box in which contributions were placed (see John 12:6; 13:29). Yet Jesus never lacked for Himself or for those who were with Him.

When Peter needed money at short notice to pay his taxes, Jesus did not tell him to go and ask Judas for money out of the box. Instead, He sent him to the Sea of Galilee to collect it from a fish's mouth (see Matthew 17:24–27). This raises an interesting question. Which would be easier: to go to the bank and cash a check or to go to the sea and cast in a hook? Certainly the latter would be much more exciting!

On another occasion, Jesus found Himself surrounded by a crowd of perhaps 12,000 hungry persons (see John 6:5–13). Taking five loaves and two fishes from a boy, He gave thanks for them to His Father. As a result, He was able to feed the whole crowd and have 12 large baskets left over. That is abundance! It is also a startling demonstration of the supernatural effects of thanking God in faith for our food!

Later, Jesus sent His disciples out to begin preaching,

but forbad them to take any extra supplies with them (see Luke 9:1–3; 10:1–4). At the end of His earthly ministry He reminded them of this and asked them whether they had lacked anything. They replied, "No, nothing" (Luke 22:35). That is abundance! I myself have served as a missionary at various times in two different countries. I know from personal observation that it is possible for a missionary to be supplied with a house, a car and a salary—and yet lack many things he needs. The key to abundance is not money or material possessions. It is faith!

Confronted by these examples from the life of Jesus, we might at first be tempted to say, "But that was Jesus! We can't expect to be like Him!" However, Jesus Himself tells us otherwise. In John 14:12 He says, "Truly, truly, I say to you, he who believes in Me, the works that I do shall he do also . . ." Likewise the apostle John, who was an eyewitness of all that Jesus did, tells us, "The one who says he abides in Him ought himself to walk in the same manner as He walked" (1 John 2:6). Jesus set the pattern for the walk of faith and we are invited to follow.

If we still hesitate to accept this challenge, it may be because we do not understand the scope of God's grace. In 2 Corinthians 9:8 the key word is *grace.* "God is able to make all *grace* abound to you . . ." The basis of our provision is not our own wisdom or ability, but God's grace. Therefore, in order to avail ourselves of it, we need to understand two key principles that govern the operation of grace.

The first principle is stated in John 1:17: "For the law was given through Moses; *grace* and truth came through Jesus Christ" (NIV). Grace has only one channel—Jesus Christ. It is not received through the observance of any legal or religious system, but solely and invariably through Christ.

The second principle is stated in Ephesians 2:8–9: "For by *grace* you have been saved *through faith* . . . not as a result of works, that no one should boast." Grace goes beyond anything that we can ever achieve or earn simply by our own ability. Therefore the only means by which we can appropriate it is *faith*. As long as we limit ourselves merely to what we deserve or what we can earn, we are failing to exercise faith and therefore we do not enjoy God's grace to the full.

How do these principles apply in the area of finance? First of all, we must emphasize that God never blesses dishonesty, laziness, or financial irresponsibility. In Proverbs 10:4 we are told, "The slack hand brings poverty, but the diligent hand brings wealth" (Jerusalem Bible). In Ephesians 4:28 Paul says, "Let him who steals steal no longer; but rather let him labor, performing with his own hands what is good, in order that he may have something to share with him who has need." God expects us, according to our ability, to engage in honest work, not merely to earn enough for ourselves, but also to have something over to share with others who are in need. In 2 Thessalonians 3:10 Paul is still more emphatic: "If anyone will not work, neither let him eat." The provision of God's grace is not offered to the dishonest or the lazy.

However, it may be that, when we have honestly and conscientiously done all in our power to provide for ourselves and our dependents, we still find ourselves on the level of bare sufficiency—or even of insufficiency. The message of grace is that we do not need to accept this as being God's will. We can turn our faith to God through Jesus Christ and trust Him to lift us—by ways of His own choosing—onto a higher level of provision

than we could ever achieve merely by our own wisdom
or ability.

God's Provision Is Corporate

Before we leave the subject of provision, there is one
more principle of great importance that we need to
recognize: *God's provision for His people is corporate.*
He does not treat us simply as isolated individuals, but
as members of a single Body, bound to one another by
strong ties of mutual commitment. In Ephesians
4:15–16, after presenting Christ as the Head of this
Body, Paul describes how God intends it to function:

> (16) from whom the whole body, being fitted
> and held together *by that which every joint
> supplies,* according to the proper working
> of each individual part, causes the growth
> of the body for the building up of itself in
> love.

Paul here emphasizes the importance of the *joints.*
They serve two functions: first, they hold the Body
together; second, they are the channels of supply.

The "joints" represent the relationships among the
various members. If these are in good order, God's
supply is able to reach every part of the Body and no
member suffers lack. But if the joints are not working
properly—that is, if the members are not rightly related
to one another—then there will be some parts of the
Body of Christ that will suffer lack. This will happen
not because God's supply is inadequate, but only
because our wrong attitudes and relationships hinder His
supply from reaching some who need it.

In the Old Testament, when God delivered Israel out

of Egypt, He taught them this principle in a very practical way. Two or three million people found themselves in a barren wilderness, without any normal food supply. To meet their need, God caused the manna to fall each night. In the morning the people had to go out and gather it before the sun caused it to melt. The actual amount that each person required was an "omer." As it worked out, some Israelites gathered more than an omer, others less. Then they shared with each other and discovered that each one had just enough—precisely one omer! (see Exodus 16:14–18). However, if they had not been willing to share in this way, some would not have had enough. Obviously God could have arranged for each individual to gather as much as he needed for himself. But He did not do so because He wanted to teach His people their responsibility for one another.

This principle carries on into the New Testament. In 2 Corinthians chapter 8, Paul is writing about a special collection he is making in the churches of Macedonia and Achaia on behalf of the poor Jewish believers in Judea. He explains to the Corinthians that this is God's way of providing equally for the various parts of the Body of Christ, without depriving some or overburdening others. To enforce this principle, he cites the example of Israel sharing their manna in the wilderness. In verses 13–15 he says:

There is no question of relieving others at the cost of hardship to yourselves; it is a question of equality. At the moment your surplus meets their need, but one day your need may be met from their surplus. The aim is equality; as Scripture has it, "The man who got much had no more than enough, and the man who got little did not go short"* (NEB).

This was how the congregation of the first Christians actually functioned in Jerusalem after the Holy Spirit was poured out upon them. In Acts 4:32–35 Luke records:

> (32)   And the congregation of those who believed were of one heart and soul; and not one of them claimed that anything belonging to him was his own; but all things were common property to them.
>
> (33)   And with great power the apostles were giving witness to the resurrection of the Lord Jesus, and abundant grace was upon them all.
>
> (34)   For there was not a needy person among them, for all who were owners of land or houses would sell them and bring the proceeds of the sales,
>
> (35)   and lay them at the apostles' feet; and they would be distributed to each, as any had need.

There are three statements here that go together. First, "the apostles were giving witness to the resurrection of the Lord Jesus." Second, "abundant grace was upon them all." Third, "there was not a needy person among them." The verbal witness of the apostles was enforced by the visible grace of God upon the believers; and the practical result was that all their needs were met. In this way the whole Body of God's people provided a single, consistent testimony to the complete sufficiency of His grace in every area of their lives.

*Paul here quotes directly from Exodus 16:18.

The world of our day needs a similar demonstration from a company of Christians who are so related to God through faith in Christ, and to one another by mutual commitment, that all their needs are met.

No Alternative to Faith

There are two sides to our relationship with God. Scripture is equally emphatic about each. On the positive side, as we have seen, God makes His abundant grace available to us on the basis of our faith. But on the negative side, God rejects any other basis on which we might seek to approach Him. Nowhere is this stated more forcefully than in Hebrews 11:6:

> (6)   And without faith it is impossible to please Him, for he who comes to God must believe that He is, and that He is a rewarder of those who seek Him.

Left to ourselves, if we were asked what we need to do to please God, few of us would offer the answer which Scripture here gives. More often than not, people try to please God on some basis other than faith: by morality, by good works, by church membership, by charitable contributions, by prayer or other religious activities. But without faith, none of these is acceptable to God. No matter what else we do, no matter how good our motives, no matter how sincere or zealous we may be, there is no substitute for faith. Without it we *cannot* please God. It is impossible!

We find ourselves therefore face to face with God's single, unvarying requirement: "he who comes to God *must believe* . . . " There are two things that we are required to believe. First, we must believe that God *is*.

Most people believe that God exists, but that by itself is not sufficient. We must also believe that God is the *rewarder of those who seek Him.* This goes beyond the fact of God's existence to His nature. We are required to believe in the essential *goodness* of God—His faithfulness and dependability. Believing in God in this way takes us beyond mere doctrine or theology. It establishes a direct, personal relationship between God and the one who believes.

In chapter 1 we said that faith relates us to two invisible objects: God and His word. Now we must go one step further. The ultimate object of faith is none other than God Himself. It is true that we believe in God's word, but we do so because His word is an extension of Himself. Our confidence in His word rests on our confidence in Himself as a Person. If we ever cease to believe in God we will eventually cease to believe His word also.

It is most important to see that merely believing a form of doctrine or theology is not the ultimate. Those whose faith goes no further than this never come to know the fullness and richness of life that God offers us. His final purpose is to bring us into an immediate, intimate, person-to-person relationship with Himself. Once established, this relationship motivates, directs, and sustains all that we do. It becomes both the source and the consummation of life. Interpreted in this way, Habakkuk's prophecy, "the righteous will live by his faith," points us not to a creed or a theology, but to an intimate, ongoing, all-embracing relationship with God Himself.

It is this kind of relationship that David speaks of in Psalm 23:1: "The LORD is my shepherd, I shall not want." David is not explaining a theology; he is describing a relationship. On the basis of his relationship to the

Lord as his Shepherd, he declares, "I shall not want."
What a marvellous expression of total personal security!
It covers every need, every situation. David could have
added other words; he could have said, "I shall not
want—money . . . or food . . . or friends . . . or
health . . ." But to do so would have weakened his
words. "I shall not want" stands best alone, leaving no
room for any lack of any kind.

I am impressed by the way in which Scripture
expresses the most profound truths in the simplest
language. In the original Hebrew, Psalm 23:1 contains
only four words. Even in the English translation, although there are nine words, only one of them contains
more than one syllable. Yet these few short words
describe a relationship so deep and so strong that it
comprehends every need that can ever arise—in life and
in death, in time and in eternity.

The Basic Sin: Unbelief

We have seen that righteousness proceeds always and
only from faith. We shall now see that the reverse also is
true: sin has only one ultimate source—unbelief.

In John 16:8 Jesus says that the ministry of the Holy
Spirit will be to convict the world concerning three
things—sin, righteousness, and judgment: "And He,
when He comes, will convict the world concerning sin,
and righteousness and judgment." Then in the next
verse Jesus defines the specific sin of which the Holy
Spirit will bring conviction: "concerning sin, because
they do not believe in Me." The primary sin, of which
the whole world is guilty, is *unbelief.* This is the basis of
all other sins.

Hebrews chapter 3 deals specifically with this sin of

unbelief. The writer reminds us that a whole generation of God's people came out of Egypt under Moses, but never entered the promised land. Instead, they perished in the wilderness.

In verse 12 the writer applies this tragic lesson from Israel to us as Christians: "Take care, brethren, lest there should be in any of you an *evil, unbelieving heart,* in falling away from the living God." Most Christians tend to view unbelief as something regrettable, but comparatively harmless. But we are here told that an *unbelieving* heart is an *evil* heart. Unbelief is evil because it causes us to fall away from God. Just as faith establishes a personal relationship with God, so unbelief destroys it. The two are exactly opposite in their effects.

In verse 13 the writer continues: "But encourage one another day after day, as long as it is still called 'Today,' lest any one of you be hardened by the deceitfulness of sin." Unbelief causes our hearts to become hardened toward God and thus exposes us to the deception of sin and of Satan. This warning against the danger of unbelief is an urgent one. The writer applies it to "Today." It concerns us Christians today no less than the Israelites who came out of Egypt under Moses. The effects of unbelief are as deadly for us as they were for them.

Finally, in verses 17 through 19 the writer sums up Israel's failure and states its cause:

> (17) And with whom was He angry for forty years? Was it not with those who sinned, whose bodies fell in the wilderness?
>
> (18) And to whom did He swear that they should not enter His rest, but to those who were disobedient?

(19) And so we see that they were not able to
enter because of unbelief.

Note the closing word—"because of *unbelief.*" These
Israelites had been guilty of many sins—fornication,
idolatry, complaining, rebellion and so on. But the
specific sin which kept them from entering their
inheritance was unbelief. Unbelief is the source of all
other sins.

This can be demonstrated logically, once we understand that true faith is based ultimately in the nature of
God Himself. If we had complete and unreserved faith
in three aspects of God's nature—His goodness, His
wisdom and His power—then we would never disobey
God. If in every situation we could believe that God is
good, that He wants only the best for us, that He has
the wisdom to know what is best and the power to
provide it, then we would never have any motive for
disobedience. So all disobedience against God, traced
back to its origin, stems from unbelief.

In the last resort, only two attitudes toward God are
possible: faith which unites us to Him, or unbelief
which separates us from Him. Each excludes the other.
In Hebrews 10:38–39 the writer once more quotes
Habakkuk's prophecy and confronts us with the two
alternatives:

(38) BUT MY RIGHTEOUS ONE SHALL LIVE
BY FAITH; AND IF HE SHRINKS BACK,
MY SOUL HAS NO PLEASURE IN HIM.
(39) But we are not of those who shrink back to
destruction, but of those who have faith to
the preserving of the soul.

Once we have committed ourselves to this life that is

based on faith, we cannot afford to turn away from it again. To go back into unbelief leads only to darkness and destruction. To go forward we must continue as we began—in faith!

Summary

The New Testament message of salvation and righteousness is based on Habakkuk 2:4: "But the righteous will live by his faith." Through faith in Jesus Christ, we receive from God, here and now, a new kind of life—divine, eternal, righteous. Thereafter, as we go on to apply our faith to the various areas of our lives, they are permeated and transformed by this new life from God.

First of all, the principle of faith must be made to work in simple, practical matters. In Romans chapter 14, Paul applies it to eating. He discusses the case of two believers who disagree about what may or may not be eaten. He concludes that what matters is not what we eat, but whether we "eat from faith."

"Eating from faith" has the following implications. First, we receive our food as a gift from God. Second, we thank God for it. Third, our food is thus "sanctified." Fourth, we devote the strength we receive from it to God's service and God's glory. In this way faith transforms the commonplace activity of eating into a sacrament.

Another practical area in which we need to apply our faith is that of financial and material provision. Through Christ, God's grace makes abundance available to us. That is, He promises to supply all our needs with something left over for others. However, abundance does not necessarily depend on money or material possessions, but solely on faith. The pattern of abundance without money or possessions is provided by Jesus Himself, and we are challenged to follow His example. At the same time we are strongly warned against laziness, dishonesty, and irresponsibility.

For all God's people to partake of His abundance, we need to see ourselves not just as isolated individuals, but as members of a single Body. God taught Israel this lesson by the manna with which He fed them in the wilderness. For each to have enough, they all had to share what they had gathered. So it is with the Body of Christ. If our attitudes and relationships are right, we share together and there is enough for all. But wrong attitudes and relationships can shut off some areas of the Body from receiving their full supply.

After the Holy Spirit was poured out on the first Christians in Jerusalem, the practical outworking of their faith was manifested in both the areas we have considered: food and finance. Their meals became sacraments, accompanied by praise and worship. They made their finances available to each other in such a way that "there was not a needy person among them." God's grace thus manifested in their daily lives helped to win their neighbors to Christ.

God offers us no alternative to faith as a basis on which to approach Him. Nor is it enough to believe simply in His existence. We must believe in His essential goodness. This takes us beyond mere theology into a direct, intimate relationship with God as a Person, which becomes our guarantee of total provision and total security.

Sin has only one ultimate source: unbelief. If we had complete, unvarying faith in God's goodness, wisdom, and power, we would never have any motive for sin. The writer of Hebrews points out that it was unbelief that kept Israel under Moses out of their inheritance and warns us as Christians against the same deadly error. In the last resort there are only two possible attitudes toward God: faith that unites us to Him or unbelief that separates us from Him.

Chapter Six

How Faith Comes

In the previous chapter we faced the challenge of God's uncompromising demands for faith: "the righteous man will live by faith . . . whatever is not from faith is sin . . . without faith it is impossible to please Him . . . he who comes to God must believe . . . " In the light of these divine demands we can easily see why Scripture compares faith to the most precious gold. Its value is unique. There is no substitute for it. Without it we cannot approach God, we cannot please Him, we cannot receive His life.

How, then, do we acquire faith? Is it something unpredictable and unexplainable over which we have no control? Or does the same Bible which presents God's demands for faith also show us the way to acquire it?

In this chapter it is my purpose to share one of the most important discoveries I ever made in the Christian life. Like most of the lessons that have proved of permanent value to me, I learned it the hard way—by personal experience. Out of a period of struggle and suffering, I eventually emerged with this one pearl of great price: *I had learned how faith comes.*

Light in a Dark Valley

During my service with the British army in World War II, I lay sick with a chronic skin infection for 12 months on end in a military hospital in Egypt. Month by month I became more and more convinced that, in that hot desert climate, the doctors did not have the means to heal me. Having recently become a Christian and been baptized in the Holy Spirit, I had a real, personal relationship with God. I felt that somehow He must have the answer to my problem—but I did not know how to find it.

Over and over again I said to myself, "I know that if I had faith, God would heal me." But then I always added, "But I don't have faith." Each time I said that, I found myself in what John Bunyan calls "the slough of despond"—the dark, lonely valley of despair. One day, however, a brilliant ray of light pierced the darkness. Propped up on my pillows in the bed, I held the King James Version of the Bible open across my knees. My eye was suddenly arrested by Romans 10:17: "So then faith cometh by hearing, and hearing by the word of God." A single word gripped my attention. It was "cometh." I laid hold of one simple fact: "Faith *cometh*!" If I did not have faith, I could get it!

But *how* does faith come? I read the verse again, "Faith cometh by hearing, and hearing by the word of God." I had already accepted the Bible as the word of God. So the source of faith was right there in my hands. But what was meant by "hearing?" How could I "hear" what the Bible had to say to me?

I determined to go back to the beginning of the Bible and read it right through, book by book in order. At the same time I armed myself with a blue pencil, intending to underline in blue every scripture that dealt with the following themes: healing; health; physical strength; long life. At times the going was not easy, but I persevered. I was surprised at how often I needed to use my blue pencil.

After about two months I had reached the book of Proverbs. There, in the fourth chapter, I found three consecutive verses that required my blue pencil:

> (20) My son, attend to my words; incline thine ear unto my sayings.
> (21) Let them not depart from thine eyes; keep them in the midst of thine heart.
> (22) For they are life unto those that find them, and health to all their flesh (Proverbs 4:20–22, KJV).

As I was underlining these words, their meaning began to open up to me. "My son . . ." It was my Father, God, speaking directly to me, His child. The message was very personal. God was telling me what His "words" and His "sayings" could be to me—"health to all my flesh." How could God promise me more for my physical body than that? "Health" and "sickness" were opposites; each excluded the other. If I could have health in "all my flesh"—my whole physical body—then there would be no room for sickness in it anywhere.

I noticed that in the margin of my Bible there was an alternative translation for "health." It was "medicine." Could God's "words" and "sayings" really be "medicine" for the healing of my whole body? After much inward debate, I determined to put it to the test. At my own request, all my medication was suspended. Then I began to take God's word as my medicine. Since I was a hospital attendant by my military trade, I was familiar with the way people usually took their medicine—"three times daily after meals." I decided to take God's word as my medicine that way.

When I made that decision, God spoke to my mind with words as clear as if I had heard them audibly: "When the doctor gives a person medicine, the directions for taking it are on the bottle. This is my medicine bottle, and the directions are on it. You had better read them."

Reading the verses carefully through once more, I saw that there were four "directions" for taking God's "medicine":

First direction: "attend . . . " I must give undivided, concentrated attention to God's words as I read them.

Second direction: "incline thine ear . . . " To incline my ear would indicate a humble, teachable attitude. I must lay aside my own prejudices and preconceptions and receive with an open mind what God was saying to me.

Third direction: "let them not depart from thine eyes . . . " I must keep my eyes focused on God's words. I must not allow them to wander to statements from other, conflicting sources, such as books or articles not based on Scripture.

Fourth direction: "keep them in the midst of thine heart . . . " Even when the actual words were no longer in front of my eyes, I must keep meditating on them in my heart, thus retaining them at the very source and center of my life.

To describe all that happened in the following months would require almost a book on its own. The army transferred me from Egypt to the Sudan, a land with one of the worst climates in Africa, where temperatures went as high as 127° F. Excessive heat always aggravated my skin condition. Everything in my circumstances was inimical to my healing. Healthy men all around me were actually becoming sick. Gradually, however, I realized that the fulfillment of God's promises does not depend on external circumstances, but solely on meeting His conditions. So I simply continued to take my "medicine" three times daily. After each main meal I bowed my head over my open Bible and said, "Lord, you have promised that these words of yours will be medicine to all my flesh. I'm taking them as my medicine now—in the name of Jesus!"

No sudden or dramatic change took place. I experienced nothing that I could describe as a "miracle." But after I had been about three months in the Sudan, I discovered that my "medicine" had made good its claims. I was perfectly well. There was no more sickness anywhere in my body. I had actually and literally received "health to all my flesh."

Nor was this a case of "mind over matter"—some kind of temporary illusion that would quickly fade. Thirty-five years have passed since then. With a few minor and brief exceptions, I have continued to enjoy excellent health. Looking back, I realize that, through that period of testing and eventual victory, I made contact with a source of life above the natural level which is still at work in my physical body today.

Logos and Rhema

I have described in some detail the steps which led me to healing and health because they illustrate certain deep, enduring principles concerning the nature of God's word. In the original Greek of the New Testament there are two different words both of which are normally translated "word." One is *logos;* the other is *rhema.* At times the two words are used interchangeably. Yet each has a distinct, special significance of its own.

The full meaning of *logos* extends beyond a word that is spoken or written. It denotes those functions which are the expression of a *mind.* The authoritative Greek lexicon of Liddell and Scott defines *logos* as "the power of the mind which is manifested in speech, *reason.*" In this sense, *logos* is the unchanging, self-existent "word of God." It is God's counsel, settled in eternity before time began, due to continue on into eternity long after time has run its course. It is of this divine *logos* that David is speaking in Psalm 119:89 when he says, "Forever, O LORD, Thy word is settled in heaven." Nothing that happens on earth can ever affect or change this word that is eternal in heaven. On the other hand, *rhema* is derived from a verb meaning to "speak," and denotes specifically a *word that is spoken*—something that occurs in time and space.

In Romans 10:17, when Paul says that "faith cometh by hearing, and hearing by the *word* of God,"* he uses the word *rhema,* not *logos.* This agrees with the fact that he couples "word" with "hearing." Logically, in order to be *heard,* a word must be *spoken.*

As I sat in my hospital bed with my Bible open across my knees, all I had in front of me—from the material point of view—was white sheets of paper with black marks imprinted upon them. But when I came to those words in Proverbs chapter 4 about God's words and sayings being health to all my flesh, they were no longer

---

*I am aware that modern translations, following texts not available to the translators of the KJV, render this verse: "So then faith comes from hearing, and hearing by the word of Christ." However, whether we read "the word of God" or "the word of Christ" makes no practical difference to the way in which faith comes. It is always God's word that comes to us through Christ (see John 14:10).

just black marks on white paper. The Holy Spirit took the very words that met my need at that moment and imparted His life to them. They became a *rhema*—something I could "hear"—a living voice speaking to my heart. It was God Himself, speaking directly and personally to me. As I heard His words, faith came to me through them.

This agrees with Paul's statement in 2 Corinthians 3:6: "the letter kills, but *the Spirit gives life.*" Apart from the Holy Spirit, there can be no *rhema*. In the Bible, the *logos*—the total counsel of God—is made available to me. But *logos* is too vast and too complex for me to comprehend or assimilate in its totality. *Rhema* is the way that the Holy Spirit brings a portion of *logos* down out of eternity and relates it to time and human experience. *Rhema* is that portion of the total *logos* that applies at a certain point in time to my particular situation. Through *rhema*, *logos* is applied to my life and thus becomes specific and personal in my experience.

In this transaction between God and man by which faith comes, the initiative is with God. This leaves no room for arrogance or presumption on our part. Indeed, in Romans 3:27 Paul tells us that boasting is excluded by the law of faith. It is God who knows—better than we do—just that part of the total *logos* which will meet our need at any given time. By His Holy Spirit He directs us to the very words that are appropriate and then imparts life to them, so that they become a *rhema*—a living voice. At this point the response required from us is "hearing." To the extent that we "hear," we receive faith.

What is involved in "hearing?" It is important that we know, as precisely as possible, what is required from us. This too was included in the lesson I received there in my hospital bed. In the wisdom of God, the words that came to me from Proverbs chapter 4 not merely met my physical need. They also provided a complete and detailed example of what it means to "hear" God's word. As God pointed out to me, the "directions" on His "medicine bottle" were fourfold: First, *attend*; second, *incline thine ear;* third, *let them not depart from thine eyes;* fourth, *keep them in the midst of thine heart.* Without at first realizing it, as I followed these four directions, I was "hearing"—and as a result, faith came.

"Hearing," then, consists of these four elements:

1. We give close, undivided attention to what God is saying to us by His Holy Spirit. By a firm decision of our will we exclude all extraneous, distracting influences.
2. We incline our ear. We adopt a humble, teachable attitude toward God. We renounce our own prejudices and preconceptions and we accept what God says in its most plain and practical meaning.
3. We focus our eyes on the words to which God has directed us. We do not allow our eyes to wander to statements from other sources that may conflict with what God is saying.
4. Even when the words are no longer before our eyes, we continue to meditate on them in our heart. In this way we retain them continually at the center of our being and their influence permeates every area of our lives.

As God's *rhema* comes to us in this way, it is both

specific and *personal.* Let me illustrate this from my experience in the hospital. God spoke to me at that time as an individual in a specific situation. He showed me how to receive my healing: I was to take His words as my medicine and forego all normal medication. I obeyed, and I was healed. However, it would have been wrong for me to assume that God would necessarily have prescribed the same remedy for someone else—or even for me at another stage of my experience. Actually, on subsequent occasions when I have needed healing, God has not always directed me in the same way. There have been times when I have gratefully accepted the help of doctors and received healing through it.

Rhema, then, comes to each of us directly and individually from God. It is appropriate to a specific time and place. It presupposes an ongoing, personal relationship with God. By each successive *rhema,* God guides us in the individual walk of faith to which He has called us. A *rhema* that is given to one believer may not be appropriate for another. Or again it may not be appropriate even for the same believer in another stage of his experience.

This life of continuing dependence upon God's *rhema* is clearly set forth in the words with which Jesus answered Satan's first temptation in the wilderness: "Man shall not live on bread alone, but on every word *(rhema)* that proceeds out of the mouth of God" (Matthew 4:4). The word "proceeds" is in the continuous present tense. We could say, " . . . every word *as it proceeds* out of the mouth of God." Jesus here speaks of a specific word proceeding directly from God's mouth, a word energized by "the breath of His mouth," which is the Holy Spirit. This is our "daily bread"— always fresh, always "proceeding." As we live in continuing dependence upon it, it imparts to us, day by day, the faith by which alone "the righteous man will live."

We may sum up the relationship between *logos* and *rhema* in the following statements:

> *Rhema* takes the eternal—*logos*—and injects it into time.
>
> *Rhema* takes the heavenly—*logos*—and brings it down to earth.
>
> *Rhema* takes the potential—*logos*—and makes it actual.
>
> *Rhema* takes the general—*logos*—and makes it specific.
>
> *Rhema* takes a portion of the total—*logos*—and presents it in a form that a man can assimilate.

Rhema is like each of the broken pieces of bread with which Jesus fed the multitude; it is suited to each individual's need and capacity; often it comes to us through another's hands.

From Heaven to Earth

In Isaiah 55:8–13 the prophet presents the relationship between *logos* and *rhema* in vivid imagery:

> (8) "For My thoughts are not your thoughts,
> Neither are your ways My ways," declares the LORD.
>
> (9) "For as the heavens are higher than the earth,
> So are My ways higher than your ways,
> And My thoughts than your thoughts.
>
> (10) "For as the rain and the snow come down from heaven,
> And do not return there without watering the earth,

And making it bear and sprout,
And furnishing seed to the sower and bread
to the eater;
(11)   So shall My word be which goes forth
from My mouth;
It shall not return to Me empty,
Without accomplishing what I desire,
And without succeeding in the matter for
which I sent it.
(12)   "For you will go out with joy,
And be led forth with peace;
The mountains and the hills will break
forth into shouts of joy before you,
And all the trees of the field will clap their
hands,
(13)   "Instead of the thornbush the cypress will
come up;
And instead of the nettle the myrtle will
come up;
And it will be a memorial to the LORD,
For an everlasting sign which will not be
cut off."

Here we have two different planes—the heavenly and
the earthly. On the heavenly plane is the divine
logos—God's ways and thoughts, the total counsel of
God, settled forever in heaven. On the earthly level are
man's ways and thoughts, far below those of God and
actually incompatible with them. There is no way by
which man can rise from his level to that of God, but
there is a way by which God's ways and thoughts can be
brought down to man. Like the rain and the snow that
bring heaven's life-giving moisture down to earth, God
says, "So shall My word be which goes forth from My
mouth."

This is the same "word" that Jesus speaks of in Matthew 4:4, "the word that proceeds out of the mouth of God," the word by which man lives. It is a portion of the heavenly *logos* coming down to earth as *rhema.* It imparts to us that portion of God's ways and thoughts which applies to our situation and meets our need at that moment.

Received and obeyed, *rhema* brings forth in our lives the activity and the fruit that glorify God. We "go out with joy," we are "led forth with peace." "Instead of the thornbush the cypress comes up, and instead of the nettle the myrtle comes up." The "thornbush" and the "nettle" typify our ways and our thoughts. As we receive the *rhema* from God's mouth, these are replaced by the "cypress" and the "myrtle," which typify God's ways and thoughts.

David and Mary, Our Examples

To further illustrate the way that *rhema* comes and the result it produces, we will take two beautiful incidents from Scripture—one from the Old Testament, concerning David, and one from the New Testament, concerning the virgin Mary.

In 1 Chronicles chapter 17 we see David established as king over Israel—victorious, prosperous, and at ease. Contrasting his own luxurious palace with the humble tabernacle that still houses the sacred ark of God's covenant, he conceives a desire to build a temple worthy of God and His covenant. The prophet Nathan, with whom David shares his desire, at first gives him warm encouragement; but the following night God speaks to Nathan and sends him back to David with a different message, which begins, "You shall not build a house for Me . . .," but closes, "Moreover, I tell you that the

LORD will build a house for you" (verses 4,10).

Here is an example of the difference between the ways and thoughts of God and of man. The highest that David in his own mind could conceive was still on the earthly plane: that he would build a house for God. The promise that came back to him from God was on the heavenly plane, far higher than David would ever have conceived: that God would build him a house. Furthermore, David had used the word "house" in its material sense, merely as a dwelling place. But God in His promise used the word in its wider meaning of an enduring posterity—a royal line that would continue forever.

In his message, Nathan had brought to David a *rhema*—a direct, personal word from God. In response, David "went in and sat before the LORD" (verse 16). What was he doing? First of all, doubtless, he had to set aside his own plans and preconceptions. Gradually, as he was emptied of these, he began to meditate with focused attention on God's message, allowing it to penetrate to his innermost being. In this condition of inner stillness, he was able to "hear." Finally, out of "hearing" faith came—the faith needed to appropriate what God had promised him. Still sitting in God's presence, David replied, "And now, O LORD, let the word that Thou hast spoken concerning Thy servant and concerning his house, be established forever, and do as Thou hast spoken" (verse 23).

"The word that Thou hast spoken"—that was the *rhema.* It did not originate on the earthly plane of David's own ways and thoughts. It came down from the heavenly place, bringing God's ways and thoughts down to David. Having "heard" this *rhema* and allowed it to produce faith within him, David appropriated its promise by a prayer that concluded with five short words: "do as Thou hast spoken." These five words represent the most effective prayer that anyone can pray—so simple, so logical, and yet irresistible in their outworking. Once we are truly convinced that God has said something to us, and we in turn ask Him to do what He has said, how can we doubt that He will do it? What power in heaven or earth can prevent it?

We move on from David through a thousand years of Jewish history to a humble descendant of his royal line—a peasant maiden named Mary in the city of Nazareth. To her appeared an angel with a message direct from the throne of God:

> (31) "And behold, you will conceive in your womb, and bear a son, and you shall name Him Jesus.
>
> (32) "He will be great, and will be called the Son of the Most High; and the Lord God will give Him the throne of His father David;
>
> (33) and He will reign over the house of Jacob forever; and His kingdom will have no end" (Luke 1:31–33).

When Mary questioned how this could come about, the angel explained that it would be by the supernatural power of the Holy Spirit, concluding with the words, "For nothing will be impossible with God" (Luke 1:37). "Nothing in the original Greek is literally "no word"—"no *rhema.*" The angel's reply could equally well be translated, "No word *(rhema)* from God shall be void of power"; or more freely, "Every word *(rhema)* from God contains the power for its own fulfillment."

The angel had brought to Mary a *rhema*—a direct, personal word from God to her. That *rhema* contained in it the power to fulfill what it promised. The outcome depended on Mary's response. "Behold, the bondslave of the Lord," she replied; "be it done to me according to your word" (Luke 1:38). By these words Mary unlocked the supernatural power of God in the *rhema* and opened herself to its fulfillment in her physical body. As a result, there occurred the greatest miracle of human history: the birth of God's eternal Son from the womb of a virgin.

In its simplicity, Mary's response was parallel to that of David. David said, "Do as Thou hast spoken." Mary said, "Be it done to me according to your word." Each of these simple replies unlocked the miracle-working power of God to fulfill the promise that had been given. In each case, the *rhema,* received by faith, contained in it the power for its own fulfillment.

Some may feel disposed to question that the miracle of the birth of Jesus depended upon the response of Mary's faith. Yet this is plainly indicated by the closing words of the salutation with which Elizabeth later greeted Mary: "And blessed is *she who believed* that there would be a fulfillment of what had been spoken to her by the Lord" (Luke 1:45). The implication is clear: the fulfillment of the promise came because Mary believed it. Without this there would have been no way for God's miracle-working power to fulfill what had been promised.

Let us see how the experiences of David and of Mary parallel each other:

> (1)   To each there came a *rhema*—a direct personal word from God.
>
> (2)   This *rhema* expressed the ways and thoughts of God—far above anything that they would ever have conceived by their

own reasoning or imagination.

(3)   As each "heard" the *rhema,* it imparted faith to him.

(4)   Each expressed his faith in a simple statement giving consent to what was promised: "Do as Thou has spoken," "Be it done to me according to your word."

(5)   Faith expressed in this way made room for the power of God within the *rhema* to bring about the fulfillment of what was promised.

God still works the same way today with His believing people. By the Holy Spirit He takes out from His eternal counsel *(logos)* a *rhema*—a specific word that fits our particular situation in time and space. As we "hear" this *rhema,* faith comes. Then as we use the faith we have thus received to appropriate the *rhema,* we discover that it contains in itself the power needed to work out its own fulfillment.

Summary

The Bible presents God's demand for faith, but it also shows us how to acquire faith. Romans 10:17 tells us that "faith comes by hearing" God's word—God's *rhema*—His word made alive and personal by the Holy Spirit.

We need to see the relationship between *logos* and *rhema. Logos* is God's unchanging counsel, settled forever in heaven. *Rhema* is the way the Holy Spirit brings a portion of *logos* down out of eternity and relates it to time and human experience. Through *rhema, logos* becomes specific and personal for me. As I hear this *rhema,* faith comes to me through it.

What is meant by "hearing?" A good, practical example is provided by Proverbs 4:20–22–God's "medicine bottle." The "directions" for taking the medicine contain the four elements that constitute "hearing": 1) We give close, undivided attention to what God is saying to us by the Holy Spirit. 2) We adopt a humble, teachable attitude. 3) We focus our eyes on the words to which God has directed us. 4) We continually meditate on them in our heart.

Rhema is God's word proceeding out of God's mouth. As we continue to hear each such word that comes to us, it provides the "daily bread" by which we maintain our spiritual life and our ongoing walk with God.

Rhema is also compared to the rain and snow which bring heaven's life-giving moisture down to earth, replacing barrenness by fruitfulness. It brings God's ways and thoughts down to our human level and replaces our ways and thoughts by His.

Two examples of how *rhema* works are provided by King David and the virgin Mary. David planned to build a house for the Lord; but the Lord sent a *rhema* that He would build a house for David. To Mary God sent a *rhema* by the angel Gabriel that she was to become the mother of Israel's long-awaited Messiah, the Son of God . In each case, as David and Mary "heard" the *rhema,* it imparted faith to them; and through faith, they were able to receive the fulfillment of what the *rhema* had promised. Their response was simple, but sufficient: "do as Thou hast spoken;" "be it done to me according to your word."

Chapter Seven

Faith Must Be Confessed

Once faith has come, there are three phases of development through which it must pass: confession, outworking, and testing. We may call these the three great "musts" of faith. Faith must be *confessed with the mouth;* faith must be *worked out in action;* faith must be *tested by tribulation.*

Confession with the Mouth

The words "confess" and "confession" are important scriptural terms with a special meaning. The Greek verb *homologeo,* normally translated to "confess," means literally "to say the same as." Thus "confession" is "saying the same as." However, translators sometimes use the related words "profess" and "profession" in place of "confess" and "confession." The phrase "profess our faith" is widely used among many Christians and is synonymous with the term used in this chapter—"confess our faith." Whichever words may be used in the English translation, the basic meaning of "confess" and "profess" remains the same: *to say the same as.*

In this special sense, "confession" is always related directly to God's word. Confession is saying the same with our mouth as God says in His word. It is making the words of our mouth agree with the written word of God.

In Psalm 116:10 the psalmist says, "I believed, therefore have I spoken" (KJV). In 2 Corinthians 4:13 Paul applies this to the confession of our faith, "But having the same spirit of faith, according to what is written, 'I BELIEVED, THEREFORE I SPOKE,' we also believe, therefore also we speak." Speaking is the natural way for faith to express itself. Faith that does not speak is stillborn.

The whole Bible emphasizes that there is a direct connection between our mouth and our heart. What happens in the one can never be separated from what happens in the other. In Matthew 12:34 Jesus tells us, "For the *mouth* speaks out of that which fills the *heart.*" Today's English Version renders this, "For the mouth speaks what the heart is full of." In other words, the mouth is the overflow valve of the heart. Whatever comes out through that overflow valve indicates the contents of the heart.

In the natural world if the water that comes from the overflow valve of a cistern contains particles of grit or fungus, then it is no good claiming that the water in the cistern is pure. There must be grit or fungus somewhere in it. So it is with the contents of our heart. If our heart is filled with faith, then that will be expressed in what we say with our mouth. But if words of doubt or unbelief come out of our mouth, they inevitably indicate that there is doubt or unbelief somewhere within our heart.

As a hospital attendant with the British forces in

North Africa during World War II, I worked for a while closely with a Scottish doctor in charge of a small field hospital that cared only for dysentery cases. Every morning as we went the round of our patients, the doctor invariably addressed each one with the same two opening sentences: "How are you? Show me your tongue!"

As I participated in this medical ritual each day, I observed that the doctor was much more interested in the state of the patient's tongue than in the answer that he received to the question, "How are you?" I have reflected many times since that the same is probably true of our relationship with God. We may offer God our own estimate of our spiritual condition, but in the last resort God, like the doctor, judges mainly from our tongue.

In Romans 10:8—10 Paul, defining the basic requirements for salvation, lays equal stress upon faith in the heart and confession with the mouth:

> (8)   But what saith it? The word is nigh thee, even in thy mouth, and in thy heart: that is, the word of faith, which we preach:
> (9)   That if thou shalt confess with thy mouth the Lord Jesus, and shalt believe in thine heart that God hath raised him from the dead, thou shalt be saved.
> (10) For with the heart man believeth unto righteousness; and with the mouth confession is made unto salvation (KJV*).

*I use the King James Version of these three verses because it is closer in structure and phraseology to the original Greek than any modern versions I have discovered.

In each of these three verses Paul speaks about the mouth and the heart, but the order in which he does so is significant. In verse 8, it is the mouth first, then the heart. In verse 9, again it is the mouth first, and then the heart. But in verse 10 the order is reversed: the heart comes first, and then the mouth.

I believe that this corresponds to our practical experience. We begin with God's word in our mouth. By confessing it with our mouth, we receive it into our heart. The more persistently we confess it with our mouth, the more firmly it becomes established in our heart. Once faith is thus established in our heart, no conscious effort is needed any longer to make the right confession. Faith naturally flows out in what we say with our mouth. Thereafter, as we continue to express our faith through our mouth, we confess our way progressively into the full benefits of salvation.

The way this process works was confirmed to me one day when I discovered that in the Hebrew language the phrase for *to learn by heart* is *to learn by mouth*. I saw that the English phrase "to learn by heart" describes the result which is to be achieved. The Hebrew phrase "to learn by mouth" describes the practical way in which we achieve that result. To learn things by heart, we repeat them over with our mouth; we go on saying them over and over, until it is no longer any effort to do so. In this way, that which begins in our mouth eventually becomes permanently imprinted in our heart.

This was how, as a boy, I learned my multiplication tables. I kept repeating them over and over: seven sevens are forty-nine; seven eights are fifty-six; seven nines are sixty-three; and so on. Eventually there was no longer any effort; there was no tendency to think or to speak otherwise. The truths of the multiplication table were indelibly imprinted on my heart. They had become a part of me. Today, more than fifty years later, you may awake me in the middle of the night with a thunderstorm raging and ask me, "What are seven sevens?" Without effort or hesitation I will reply, "Forty-nine."

In the same way we may have the word of God indelibly imprinted on our heart. Each time a need arises, or our faith is challenged, we confess God's word as it applies to that situation. At first, there may be a struggle. Our feelings may prompt us to say something that does not agree with God's word. But we persistently resist our feelings and make the words of our mouth agree with God's word. Eventually there will be no more struggle. It will be natural for us to say with our mouth, concerning each situation, the same that God says in His word.

It is essential to distinguish between faith and feeling. Feeling is based on our senses. Many times its conclusions are contrary to God's word. But faith, as we have already seen, relates us to the invisible realm of God and His word. Wherever faith and feeling come into conflict, we must determine that, by our confession, we will take our stand with faith, not with feeling.

There are three words, each beginning with "f," that we must put in their right order: fact—faith—feeling. The *facts* are found in the word of God, and they never vary. *Faith* takes its stand with the facts of God's word, and confesses them as true. *Feelings* may waver; but ultimately, if faith stands fast, feelings will come into line with the facts. On the other hand, if we start at the wrong end—with feeling rather than fact—we will always end up in trouble. Our feelings change hour by hour and moment by moment. If our life is based on them, it will be as unstable as they are. "The righteous man shall live by faith"—not by feelings!

Five Practical Safeguards

This practice of persistently making the right confession with our mouth is very effective and very powerful. However, if perverted, it can lead to abuses which are spiritually dangerous. For instance, it may degenerate into a "mind-over-matter" type of approach. Such an approach was taught by the French philosopher Coue, whose remedy for life's problems was to keep repeating, "Every day and in every way I'm getting better and better."Another danger is that a zealous but immature Christian may imagine that he has found a way to "twist God's arm" and compel the Almighty to meet his demands. Or again, our concept of God may be reduced to a kind of heavenly "Vending Machine," which only needs the right coin in the right slot to deliver the particular brand of carnal satisfaction that we select.

To avoid abuses of this kind, I would suggest five scriptural safeguards:

First Safeguard: We need to examine the attitude with which we approach God. The writer of Hebrews makes the following comments about the prayer which Jesus offered in the garden at Gethsemane: "he was heard because of his reverent submission"(Hebrews 5:7, NIV). Jesus' attitude of "reverent submission" was expressed in the words, "yet not My will, but Thine be done" (Luke 22:42). This sets a pattern that we all must follow. Until we renounce our own will and submit to God's, we have no scriptural basis upon which to claim the answers to our prayers or the benefits of our salvation.

Second Safeguard: We are not free to "confess" just anything that we ourselves arbitrarily imagine or desire. Our confession must be kept *within the limits of God's written word.* Any kind of confession that is not based directly on Scripture can easily develop into wishful thinking or fanaticism.

Third Safeguard: We never cease to be dependent on the leading of the Holy Spirit. In Romans 8:14 Paul defines those who qualify to be recognized as "the sons of God": "For all who are being *led by the Spirit of God,* these are *sons of God."* This applies as much to the confession that we make with our mouth as to any other aspect of the Christian life. The Holy Spirit must lead us to the particular area of scriptural truth which we need to confess in any given situation. In the previous chapter, we saw that only the Holy Spirit can take the eternal *logos* and apply it to each situation as a living, practical *rhema.*

Fourth Safeguard: We never cease to be dependent on God's supernatural grace. In Ephesians 2:8 Paul states an order that never varies: "by grace . . . through faith . . ." It is always *grace* first, then *faith.* If we ever cease to depend on God's grace and power, and begin to rely on our own ability, the result in our experience will be the same as it was in Abraham's—an Ishmael, not an Isaac.

Fifth Safeguard: It is important to evaluate correctly the evidence of our own senses. God does not ask us to close our eyes and ears and walk about as though the physical, material world around us does not exist. Faith is not mysticism. We do not question the *reality* of what our senses reveal, but we do question its *finality.*

In Romans 4:16–21 Paul begins by emphasizing that valid faith must always depend on God's grace, and then he sets forth Abraham as an example of how to resolve the tension between faith and the senses:

> (16) Therefore, the promise comes *by faith, so that it may be by grace* and may be guaran-

teed to all Abraham's offspring—not only to those who are of the law but also to those who are of the faith of Abraham. He is the father of us all.

(17) As it is written: "I have made you a father of many nations." He is our father in the sight of God, in whom he believed—the God who gives life to the dead and calls things that are not as though they were.

(18) Against all hope, Abraham in hope believed and so became the father of many nations, just as it had been said to him, "So shall your offspring be."

(19) Without weakening in his faith, he faced the fact that his body was as good as dead—since he was about a hundred years old—and that Sarah's womb was also dead.

(20) Yet he did not waver through unbelief regarding the promise of God, but was strengthened in his faith and gave glory to God,

(21) being fully persuaded that God had power to do what he had promised (NIV).

Abraham's senses told him that he was physically incapable of begetting a child and that Sarah was likewise incapable of bearing one. Yet God had promised them a son of their own. Abraham did not pretend that what his senses revealed to him about his own body and about Sarah's was not *real.* He simply refused to accept it as *final.* When God's word promised him one thing and his senses told him another, he clung tenaciously to God's promise, without letting his senses cause him to doubt that promise. Finally, after their faith had been tested, the physical condition both of

Abraham's body and of Sarah's was brought into line with what God had promised, and they became actually, physically capable of having a child.

It will be the same with us. There may be a period of conflict between the statements of God's word and what our senses tell us about a particular situation. But if our faith is valid, and if we cling on to it as Abraham did, steadfastly maintaining the right confession, in due course the physical condition confronting us through our senses will be brought into line with what God's word has to say about it.

Confessing unto Salvation

We have seen that Paul concludes his teaching in Romans 10:8–10 with the statement "with the mouth confession is made *unto salvation.*" The word "unto" indicates motion, or progress. In other words, we move progressively forward into salvation as we continue making the right confession.

However, in order to make and maintain the right confession, we need to understand the scope of the word "salvation." Many Christians limit "confession" to confessing their sins and "salvation" to having their sins forgiven. It is true that God does require us to confess our sins and that salvation includes having our sins forgiven. But the scope of both confession and salvation goes far beyond this.

In Psalm 78:21–22 we are told that God became angry with Israel after their deliverance from Egypt, "Because they did not believe in God, And did not trust in His salvation." The verses that precede and that follow make it clear that God's "salvation" included all that He had done for Israel up to that point: His judgments upon the Egyptians; the parting of the Red Sea; the cloud to guide them by day and the fire by night; the water that came from the rock for them to drink and the manna that came from heaven for them to eat. These, and all God's other acts of intervention and provision on their behalf, are summed up in the single, all-inclusive word "salvation."

In the New Testament, too, the Greek verb *sozo*—usually translated to "save"—goes far beyond the forgiveness of sins and includes the meeting of every human need. To give but a few examples of its wider meaning, *sozo* is used for: the healing of the woman with an issue of blood (Matthew 9:21–22); the healing of the cripple at Lystra, lame from his mother's womb (Acts 14:8–10); the deliverance of the Gadarene demoniac from a legion of demons and his being restored to his right mind (Luke 8:36); the raising of the daughter of Jairus from the dead (Luke 8:49–55); the prayer of faith restoring the sick to health (James 5:15).

Finally, in 2 Timothy 4:18 Paul said, "The Lord will deliver me from every evil deed, and will *bring me safely* to His heavenly kingdom . . ." The word here translated to "bring safely" is *sozo*. In this context, it included every deliverance, protection, and provision of God needed to take Paul safely through his earthly life and to bring him finally into God's eternal kingdom.

Salvation, then, comprehends the total benefits purchased for us by the death of Christ on the cross. Whether these benefits are spiritual, physical, financial, material, temporal, or eternal, they are all summed up in one great, all-inclusive word—"salvation."

The way by which we enter into and appropriate the various benefits of salvation is "confession." Scripture gives us clear, positive statements by which to lay hold of every area of God's provision. As we receive these by faith in our heart and confess them with our mouth, we make them ours in actual experience.

For instance, Satan often assails Christians with feelings of condemnation and unworthiness. We may even begin to question God's love for us. We need to overcome these satanic assaults by finding and confessing the scriptures that will silence our accuser. For example:

> There is therefore now no condemnation for those who are in Christ Jesus (Romans 8:1).

> But God demonstrates His own love toward us, in that while we were yet sinners, Christ died for us (Romans 5:8).

> And we have come to know and have believed the love which God has for us (1 John 4:16).

On the basis of these scriptures, I make the following personal confession: "I am in Christ Jesus; therefore I am not under condemnation . . . God proved His love for me by the fact that Christ died for me while I was still a sinner . . . I know and believe the love that God has for me . . ." As I resist all negative feelings and maintain this positive, scriptural confession, condemnation and rejection are replaced in my experience by peace and acceptance.

Or our need may be in the area of physical healing and health. Scripture tells us, concerning Jesus, "HE

HIMSELF TOOK OUR INFIRMITIES, AND CARRIED AWAY OUR DISEASES" (Matthew 8:17); "for by His wounds you were healed" (1 Peter 2:24). These statements provide the basis for the confession that is appropriate in this area. Every time sickness threatens, instead of letting my mind dwell on the symptoms, I respond with a positive confession: "Jesus Himself took my infirmities and carried away my diseases, and by His wounds I was healed." At first I may waver, caught in the tension between the symptoms of my physical body and the unchanging truths of God's word. But as I continue to confess God's truth, it becomes a part of me—just like the multiplication table. Even if I wake up in the middle of the night with the symptoms of three different diseases in my body, my spirit still makes the right confession: "By His wounds I was healed."

If my need is in yet another area, then I make the confession that is appropriate to that area. For instance, if I am going through a period of financial shortage, I remind myself of 2 Corinthians 9:8:"And God is able to make all grace abound to you, that always having all sufficiency in everything, you may have an abundance for every good deed . . ." I refuse to entertain my fears. I conquer fear by thanksgiving. I continue to thank God that the revealed level of His provision for me is abundance. As I maintain this confession, I see God intervene in such a way that the truth of His word is made real in my financial situation.

Thus progressively—area by area, need by need, situation by situation—"confession is made unto salvation." Each problem that we encounter becomes a stimulus to make the confession that declares God's answer to that problem. The more complete and consistent our confession, the more fully we enter into the experiential enjoyment of our salvation.

The High Priest of Our Confession

One major, distinctive theme that runs through the epistle to the Hebrews is the high priesthood of Jesus Christ. In this capacity, Jesus ministers as our personal representative in the presence of God the Father. He covers us with His righteousness, offers up our prayers, presents our needs, and becomes surety for the fulfillment of God's promises on our behalf. However, as we trace this theme of Christ's high priesthood through the epistle, we discover that it is invariably linked with our confession. The confession that we make on earth determines the extent to which Jesus is free to exercise His priestly ministry on our behalf in heaven.

In Hebrews 3:1 we are exhorted to consider Jesus Christ as "the High Priest of our confession." This links Christ's high priesthood directly to our confession. It is our confession that makes His priestly ministry effective on our behalf. Each time we make the right confession, we have the whole authority of Christ as our high priest behind us. He becomes surety for the fulfillment of that which we confess. But if we fail to make the right confession, or if we confess doubt or unbelief rather than faith, then we give Christ no opportunity to minister as our high priest. Right confession invokes His priestly ministry on our behalf, but wrong confession shuts us off from it.

In Hebrews 4:14 the writer again links the high priesthood of Jesus directly to our confession: "Since then we have a great high priest who has passed through the heavens, Jesus the Son of God, let us hold fast our confession." The emphasis here is on *holding fast* our confession. Once we have brought the words of our mouth into agreement with God's written word, we must be careful not to change or go back to a position of unbelief. Many pressures may come against us. It may seem that things are going exactly contrary to what we could have expected. All natural sources of help may fail. But by our faith and our confession we must continue to hold on to those things which do not change—to the word of God and to Jesus Christ as our high priest at God's right hand.

In Hebrews 10:21–24, for the third time, the writer stresses the connection between Christ's high priesthood and our confession:

> (21) And since we have a great priest over the house of God,
>
> (22) let us draw near with a sincere heart in full assurance of faith, having our hearts sprinkled clean from an evil conscience and our body washed with pure water.
>
> (23) Let us hold fast the confession of our hope without wavering, for He who promised is faithful;
>
> (24) and let us consider how to stimulate one another to love and good deeds.

We see that the recognition of Jesus as our high priest places upon us three successive obligations, each introduced by the words "let us . . ." The first (in verse 22) relates to God: we are to "draw near with a sincere heart . . ." The second (in verse 23) concerns our own confession: we are to "hold fast the confession of our hope without wavering . . ." The third (in verse 24) relates to our fellow believers: we are to "consider how to stimulate one another to love and good deeds . . ." Central to our obligations toward God and toward our fellow believers is our obligation to ourselves: to hold fast the right confession. The measure in which we do this will determine the measure in which we will be able to fulfill our other two obligations—to God and to our fellow believers.

In the three passages of Hebrews we have looked at, there is a mounting emphasis upon the importance of maintaining a right confession. In Hebrews 3:1 we are told simply that Jesus is "the high priest of our confession." In Hebrews 4:14 we are exhorted to *"hold fast our confession."* In Hebrews 10:23 we are exhorted to hold fast our confession *"without wavering."* The suggestion is that we are likely to be subjected to ever-increasing pressures that would cause us to change or weaken our confession. Many of us could testify that this is true to our experience. Therefore the warning is timely. No matter what may be the pressures against us, victory comes only through holding fast our confession.

In the last of these three exhortations in Hebrews, the writer gives us a specific reason why we should hold fast and not waver. He adds, "for He who promised is faithful." Our confession links us to a high priest who cannot change. It is the God-appointed means by which we invoke on our behalf His faithfulness, His wisdom, and His power.

Summary

In God's plan of salvation, faith is linked directly to confession. "Confession" (or "profession") means that we systematically make the words of our mouth agree with the written word of God. This requires continuing self-discipline. In each situation that confronts us we refuse to be swayed by our feelings or our senses, but we resolutely reaffirm what Scripture has to say about such a situation. At first there may be struggle and tension, but ultimately the word of God becomes indelibly imprinted on our heart, and thereafter it flows out naturally through our mouth.

We must be careful that the practice of confession does not degenerate into a mere "technique." The following are five practical safeguards:

(1) We must begin by renouncing our own will and submitting to God's.

(2) We must keep our confession based strictly on Scripture.

(3) We must be continually led by the Holy Spirit.

(4) We must always rely on God's supernatural grace, never merely on our own natural ability.

(5) Where there is a conflict between our senses and God's word, we must take the same stand as Abraham: conditions revealed by our senses are *real,* but not *final.*

As we progressively apply the right confession to every area of our lives, we move forward into an ever fuller experience of "salvation"–that is, God's total provision obtained for us by the death of Christ.

Right confession links us directly to Christ as our high priest in God's presence, and invokes on our behalf His unchanging faithfulness, wisdom, and power.

Chapter Eight

Faith Must Be Worked Out

Faith, we have seen, must be confessed with the mouth. But is that all? So often religious people are guilty of using empty words without real meaning. How can we avoid this? How can we be sure that the words we use in our confession really proceed from genuine faith in our heart? To this question Scripture gives a simple, practical answer: Faith that is confessed with the mouth must be backed up by appropriate actions. Faith without works—that is, without appropriate actions—is dead.

Faith Works by Love

In Galatians 5:6 Paul goes to the heart of the matter: "For in Christ Jesus neither circumcision nor uncircumcision means anything, but faith working through love." Paul here establishes four vital points which follow each other in logical order.

First, taking circumcision as an example, Paul says that no outward ritual or ceremony can by itself commend us to God. God is primarily concerned with the internal, not the external.

Secondly, the one essential element in true Christianity is *faith*. This is the inner condition of the heart which alone is acceptable to God and for which there is no substitute. In chapter 5 we have already noted the Bible's insistent emphasis on the necessity and centrality of faith.

Thirdly, Paul tells us, faith *works*. It is the very nature of faith to be active. Where there is no appropriate activity, there is no genuine faith.

Fourthly, the way in which faith naturally acts is by *love*. Where there is no love manifested, there is no genuine faith. Love is essentially positive, strengthening, comforting, upbuilding. Where actions are all negative, critical, uncharitable, there is no evidence of love and therefore none of faith. Such actions may perhaps proceed from religion, but certainly not from faith.

One book of the New Testament which emphasizes the relationship between faith and works is the Epistle of James. Some commentators suggest that there is a difference between James' view of faith and Paul's view of faith. They say that Paul emphasizes salvation by faith alone, without works, while James asserts that faith must be expressed by works. Personally, I find no contradiction: only two obverse sides of the same truth. We are justified by faith without works, because there are no works we can do that will earn us righteousness. But once we are justified by faith without works, we must then express our faith by our works, or else our faith is not valid. So Paul tells us *how* we receive righteousness from God and James tells us what results follow *when* we receive righteousness from God. I see no conflict between these two views: only a difference in emphasis.

Furthermore, it is completely wrong to suggest that Paul lays no emphasis upon works. In Galatians 5:6, as we have already seen, he shows that the very nature of faith is to work—and to work through love. He brings out the same truth also in the famous thirteenth chapter of First Corinthians—the "love" chapter—and in many other places in his writings.

James Emphasizes Works

The main part of James' teaching concerning faith and works is contained in his epistle, chapter 2, verses 14–26. We will divide this passage up into six main sections and analyze each in order.

Section 1, verses 14–17: Confession without Action

(14)   What use is it, my brethren, if a man says he has faith, but he has no works? Can that faith save him?

(15)   If a brother or sister is without clothing and in need of daily food,

(16)   and one of you says to them, "Go in peace, be warmed and be filled"; and yet you do not give them what is necessary for their body; what use is that?

(17)   Even so faith, if it has no works, is dead, being by itself.

We need to see that James is here describing a man who *says* he has faith. In other words, the man claims to have faith, but his behavior belies his claim. Confronted by a fellow believer in desperate physical need, this man merely offers words of comfort, but does nothing practical to help. His failure to act in the appropriate way shows that his words of comfort were empty and insincere. The same applies to our profession—or confession—of faith. If it is not followed by appropriate actions, then all we have is a lifeless form of words, without any inner reality.

Section 2, verse 18: Theology vs. Life

> (18)   But someone may well say, "You have faith, and I have works; show me your faith without the works, and I will show you my faith by my works."

I always accept this verse as a personal challenge. Do I have a faith which is a mere abstract theology, or do I demonstrate what I believe by what I do? The world has grown tired of faith presented as an abstract diagram, but is eager to see it in the form of a working model. My personal conviction is that a theology which does not work in practice is not valid.

Section 3, verse 19: The Devil's Orthodoxy

> (19)   You believe that God is one. You do well; the demons also believe, and shudder.

It is highly orthodox to believe that there is only one true God. But it is not enough. Even the demons believe that—and shudder! I am convinced that the devil himself believes the whole Bible. He is much more orthodox than many theologians! What, then, is missing in faith such as this? The answer can be given in one word: *Obedience!* Although Satan and his demons believe in one true God, they persist in their rebellion against Him. *True faith leads to submission and obedience.* Otherwise it is vain!

Section 4, verses 20–24: The Example of Abraham

> (20)   But are you willing to recognize, you fool-
> ish fellow, that faith without works is
> useless?
>
> (21)   Was not Abraham our father justified by
> works, when he offered up Isaac his son on
> the altar?
>
> (22)   You see that faith was working with his
> works, and as a result of the works, faith
> was perfected;
>
> (23)   and the Scripture was fulfilled which says,
> "AND ABRAHAM BELIEVED GOD, AND
> IT WAS RECKONED TO HIM AS RIGHT-
> EOUSNESS," and he was called the friend
> of God.
>
> (24)   You see that a man is justified by works,
> and not by faith alone.

James now turns to the life of Abraham to illustrate
his point. To follow what he is saying, we need to look
at some of the main incidents in Abraham's life. In
Genesis chapter 12 God called Abraham to leave Ur of
the Chaldees in order to go to a land which he was to
receive as an inheritance. When Abraham obeyed, God
led him to the land of Canaan. In Genesis chapter 15
Abraham complained to God that he still had no heir,
born of his own body, to inherit the land. In reply, God
showed him the stars at night and said, "So shall your
descendants be." Abraham's response is recorded in
Genesis 15:6: "Then he believed in the LORD; and He
reckoned it to him as righteousness." At this point God
reckoned Abraham as being righteous, not on the basis
of any good works that he had done, but solely because
he had believed God.

However, James points out, this was not the end of

Abraham's faith relationship to God. Having believed
God and had righteousness reckoned to him on the basis
of faith alone, Abraham then went on to work out his
faith in a whole series of actions that followed. In the
next seven chapters of Genesis we find that God led
Abraham step by step, in one act of obedience after
another, gradually maturing his faith over a period of
about 40 years. Finally, in Genesis chapter 22, Abraham
came to the point where he could face the supreme test
of his faith: the offering up of his son Isaac on God's
altar. This he did, according to Hebrews 11:17–19,
being fully persuaded that God would bring Isaac back
to life again. Thus he emerged triumphant from the
test.

Abraham was not ready to meet such a test as this in
Genesis chapter 15. It took many preparatory tests and
struggles, many successive acts of obedience, to bring
him to this climax where he was willing to offer up
Isaac. James explains this by saying that "faith was
working with his works, and as a result of the works,
faith was perfected." Faith is always the starting point.
There can be no other. Once faith has come into being,
it is then worked out in successive tests which it meets
with appropriate acts of obedience. Each act of obedience develops and strengthens faith and thus prepares it
for the next test. Finally, through a whole series of such
tests and acts of obedience, faith is brought to maturity,
or perfection.

Section 5, verse 25: The Example of Rahab

(25)   And in the same way was not Rahab the
harlot also justified by works, when she
received the messengers and sent them out
by another way?

For his final example of the relationship between faith and works James turns to Rahab. The story of Rahab is recorded in Joshua 2:1−22 and 6:21−25. One reason why I enjoy her story is that it proves there is hope for the hopeless. Rahab was a sinful, heathen woman, living in Jericho, a city doomed by God to destruction. Yet because of her faith she escaped destruction, saved her entire household, was incorporated into God's people and married a man who−together with her−is named as an ancestor of Jesus Christ (see Matthew 1:5).

However, Rahab's faith was not an empty profession, but was expressed in appropriate actions. The spies sent into Jericho by Joshua lodged in her house. When they faced capture, she risked her life to save them by hiding them on the roof. Before the spies left, Rahab struck a bargain with them: "I have saved your lives. In turn, I ask you to save me and my household." The spies agreed and pledged themselves to do what Rahab asked. Actually they made this pledge on behalf of God rather than on their own behalf, since it was God Himself who brought about the destruction of Jericho by supernatural power (see Joshua 6:20). With the bargain made, Rahab once again risked her life by letting the spies down from her window on a rope.

Before the spies left, they gave Rahab one final instruction: "If you want to be saved, tie this scarlet thread to your window. If the thread is not in the window, you will not be saved." The scarlet thread was a form of confession. By it Rahab visibly showed her faith in the spies' promise. For us, in the light of the New Testament, it beautifully represents our confession of faith in the blood of Christ.

Rahab's story vividly illustrates the relationship that

draws together faith, confession, and appropriate action. Rahab *believed* the testimony of the spies that Jericho would be destroyed. She also *believed* their promise to save her and her household. But that was not enough. She had to *confess* her faith by placing the scarlet thread in the window. But that, too, was not enough. She had to *act out* her faith, even at the risk of her own life, by first hiding the spies on her roof and then letting them down from her window. It was appropriate that the scarlet thread was to be placed in that very window. The thread in the window would not have saved her if she had not also used the window to save the spies. Rahab's story illustrates three things that must never be separated from one another: faith, confession, and appropriate action.

Section 6, verse 26: Conclusion

> (26) For just as the body without the spirit is dead, so also faith without works is dead.

James concludes his analysis with a blunt, but vivid analogy: faith without works is a corpse. It may perhaps be a mummy, solemnly preserved in a religious setting, but for all that, it is dead. The only thing that can give life to a body is the spirit. Likewise, the only thing that can give life to faith is works—appropriate actions.

Faith Is a Walk

In the foregoing analysis we saw how James used Abraham as his primary example of faith combined with works. In Romans 4:11—12 Paul also sets Abraham before us as a pattern of faith that we should follow:

(11)   And he received the sign of circumcision, a seal of the righteousness of the faith which he had while uncircumcised, that he might be the father of all who believe without being circumcised, that righteousness might be reckoned to them,

(12)   and the father of circumcision to those who not only are of the circumcision, but who also follow in the steps of the faith of our father Abraham which he had while uncircumcised.

First, Paul explains that Abraham was not made righteous by the act of circumcision. Rather, he received circumcision as an outward seal of the righteousness which had already been reckoned to him on the basis of faith alone. The inference is that circumcision, unless based on faith, is of no value by itself.

Then Paul goes on to say that Abraham, by his example of faith, became the father of all subsequent believers, whether circumcised or uncircumcised. However, Paul also lays down a condition which we must all fulfill, regardless of racial or religious background, if we claim to be reckoned as Abraham's descendants. It is that we "also follow in the steps of the faith of our father Abraham which he had while uncircumcised."

Paul speaks about "the steps of Abraham's faith." This is a vivid picture, illustrating that faith is not static. It is not a condition, or a position. Rather it is a progressive walk that we take step by step. Each step springs out of our personal relationship with God. For this reason we cannot make all-embracing rules as to how every believer should act. Different believers are in different stages of the faith walk. A believer who has been in the faith many years should be further down the road than a new convert. What God requires of a mature believer is different from what He requires of a beginner. In my personal faith walk, I must take the step that expresses my relationship with God at that moment. I cannot necessarily take the same steps as other believers who are more or less mature than I am.

Faith, then, is a walk—the outcome of an ongoing personal relationship between God and each believer. Every step in that walk is an act of obedience. As we thus walk in a right relationship with God, worked out in progressive acts of obedience, our faith is developed and finally brought to maturity.

Summary

The confession of our faith must be accompanied by appropriate acts, motivated by love. Without these, faith is vain.

The Epistle of James establishes three principles governing the relationship between faith and works: 1) Confession without action is worthless. 2) Theology must be made to work in practical living. 3) Orthodoxy must be accompanied by obedience.

James illustrates these principles by two Old Testament examples: 1) Abraham had righteousness reckoned to him by God on the basis of faith alone; but thereafter his faith was developed and matured by progressive acts of obedience, culminating in the offering of his son Isaac on God's altar. 2) Rahab not merely believed the spies' report; she risked her life to save them and confessed her faith in their promise by the scarlet thread in her window, thus combining faith, confession, and appropriate action.

In summary, James declares that faith without works is as lifeless as a body without a spirit.

Paul, in turn, uses the example of Abraham to demonstrate that faith is not a static condition, but a progressive walk, arising out of a personal relationship with God. Each step in this walk is an act of obedience. Through a whole series of such steps, faith is developed and finally brought to maturity.

Chapter Nine

Faith Must Be Tested

We have seen that faith must be confessed with the mouth and must be worked out in action. Now we come to the third "must." This is the one we usually do not like to face. Nevertheless, we cannot avoid it: faith must be *tested.*

Exulting in Tribulation

In Romans 5:1–11, speaking of our faith relationship with God through Christ, Paul uses the word "exult" three times. This is a very strong word, denoting a confidence which actually causes us to boast.

In verse 2 Paul says, "we *exult* in hope of the glory of God." This is not difficult to understand. If we really believe that we are even now heirs of God's glory and that we are going to share it with Him throughout eternity, it is natural to feel and to express excitement and joyful anticipation.

But in verse 3 Paul uses precisely the same word again and he says, "And not only this, but we also *exult* in our tribulations. " At first sight, this seems ridiculous.

Who could ever imagine exulting in tribulations—in hardship, persecution, loneliness and misunderstanding, or in poverty, sickness, and bereavement? Why should Paul suggest, or God expect, that we should exult in such things as these?

Fortunately, Paul gives us a reason, for he continues: "knowing that tribulation brings about perseverance; and perseverance, proven character; and proven character, hope; and hope does not disappoint; because the love of God has been poured out within our hearts through the Holy Spirit who was given to us" (verses 3–5). To sum up Paul's answer, the reason for exulting even in tribulation is that, when received as from God and endured in faith, it produces results in our character which cannot be produced in any other way.

Analyzing Paul's answer in detail, we find that he lists four successive stages in character development that result from meeting the test of tribulation. They are:

First, *perseverance.* An alternative translation would be *endurance.* This is an essential aspect of Christian character. Without it, we will not be able to enter into many of God's choicest blessings and provisions for us.

Second, *proven character.* The Greek word here translated is *dokime.* Some alternative translations given in other modern versions are: "strength of character" (Living Bible); "a mature character" (J.B. Phillips); "God's approval" (Jerusalem Bible); "proof that we have stood the test" (New English Bible). The word is closely associated with metal that has stood the test of the crucible—a picture to which we will return shortly.

Third, *hope.* J.B. Phillips renders this "a steady hope." This is not mere daydreaming, or wishful thinking, or flights of fancy that are an escape from reality. Hope of this kind is a strong, serene, confident expectation of good—the good that will ultimately result from the process of testing.

Fourth, *the love of God* poured out in our hearts, which, so far from being a disappointment, far exceeds any hope we could ever have entertained. Thus the final objective of God in dealing with our character is to bring us into the enjoyment of His own divine love.

Moving on to verse 11, we come to Paul's third use of the word *exult:* "And not only this, but we also *exult in God* through our Lord Jesus Christ . . . " Here again, we have a divine objective. God is not satisfied that our joy or our confidence should rest merely in what He has done for us, no matter how wonderful His blessings, His gifts, and His provisions may be. God's purpose is that we should find our final and highest satisfaction in nothing and in no one but Himself. Without the process of character development already outlined, this would not be possible. It is a sure mark of spiritual maturity when God Himself, and God alone, becomes both the source of our deepest joy and the object of our highest devotion.

It is interesting to compare Paul's teaching here in Romans chapter 5 with his teaching in 1 Corinthians chapter 13, the famous chapter on divine love. In Romans, Paul shows us that the way to enter into the fullness of divine love is by perseverance, or endurance. In 1 Corinthians 13:7 he puts it the other way round. He tells us that love is the only thing strong enough to endure every test: "love . . . bears all things, believes all things, hopes all things, *endures all things."* Scripture thus forges a bond which cannot be severed between *love* and *endurance.*

Again, in Romans chapter 5, Paul presents faith, hope, and love as three successive phases of Christian experience: faith leads to hope, and hope leads to love.

In 1 Corinthians 13:13 he presents the same three qualities in the same order, but he emphasizes that, while each is of permanent value, love is the greatest: "But now abide faith, hope, love, these three; but the greatest of these is love." As we contemplate these three beautiful qualities in the mirror of God's word, we need to keep the eyes of our heart fastened upon them until they become an enduring part of our own character. In this way the truth of 2 Corinthians 3:18 is worked out in our experience: "But we all, with unveiled face beholding as in a mirror the glory of the Lord, are being transformed into the same image from glory to glory, just as from the Lord, the Spirit." "From glory to glory" means, in part at least, from faith to hope, and from hope to love.

In his epistle chapter 1, verses 2–4, James sets out the same pattern of faith being developed by testing:

> (2) Consider it all joy, my brethren, when you encounter various trials;
>
> (3) knowing that the testing of your faith produces endurance.
>
> (4) And let endurance have its perfect result, that you may be perfect and complete, lacking in nothing.

Paul tells us that we are to *exult* in tribulations; James tells us that we are to count all our trials as *joy*. Each is equally contrary to our natural thinking, but each has the same reason: testing—and testing alone—can produce endurance, and endurance is the only way that we can enter into the fullness of God's will for us. James expresses this by saying, "that you may be perfect and complete, lacking in nothing." With such an end as this in view, we have a logical reason to accept the testing of our faith joyfully.

Tested by Fire

Like Paul and James, Peter too warns us of the trials that our faith must undergo. In 1 Peter 1:5 he describes Christians as those "who are protected by the power of God *through faith* for a salvation ready to be revealed in the last time." He emphasizes that it is only *through our faith* that God's power can work effectively in our lives; and therefore that continuing faith is an essential requirement for participating in the full and final revelation of God's salvation. Then, in the next two verses, he describes how our faith will be tested:

> (6)   In this [i.e., the expectation of salvation] you greatly rejoice, even though now for a little while, if necessary, you have been distressed by various trials,
>
> (7)   that the proof of your faith, being more precious than gold which is perishable, even though tested by fire, may be found to result in praise and glory and honor at the revelation of Jesus Christ.

Peter here compares the testing of our faith to the way in which, at that period, gold was tested—and purified—by fire in a furnace. He returns to the same theme in 1 Peter 4:12–13:

> (12)   Beloved, do not be surprised at the fiery ordeal among you, which comes upon you for your testing, as though some strange thing were happening to you;

(13)   but to the degree that you share the sufferings of Christ, keep on rejoicing.

At first, as we pass through "the fiery ordeal," we
may interpret it as "some strange thing," something
which does not belong to the Christian life. But Peter
assures us that, on the contrary, testing of this kind is a
necessary part of that life, essential for the purifying of
our faith just as fire is essential for the purifying of gold.
Therefore he exhorts us to "keep on rejoicing." Again
we find in the teaching of Peter, as we have found in
that of Paul and James, the seeming paradox of intense
testing associated with intense joy.

In Malachi 3:2–3 the prophet paints a vivid picture
of Jesus, as the long-awaited Messiah, coming to His
people and dealing with them as a refiner deals with
gold and silver:

(2)   "But who can endure the day of His
coming? And who can stand when He
appears? For He is like a refiner's fire and
like fullers' soap.

(3)   "And He will sit as a smelter and purifier of
silver, and He will purify the sons of Levi
and refine them like gold and silver, so that
they may present to the Lord offerings in
righteousness."

In purifying gold and silver, the refiner of Bible times
suspended the metal, in a melting pot, over the hottest
fire that he could produce. He usually built the fire in
some form of clay oven and used bellows to fan the
flame. As the metal seethed in the pot, the "dross"—
that is, the various impurities—was forced to the surface

and was skimmed off by the refiner (see Proverbs 25:4). This process continued until all impurities had been removed and nothing but the pure, refined metal was left.

It has been said that the refiner, bending over the metal in his pot, was not satisfied of its complete purity until he could see his own image accurately reflected in its surface. In the same way, the Lord, as our refiner, continues to apply the fires of testing to us until He sees His own image reflected without distortion from our lives.

Trials or afflictions are the crucible in which God refines and purifies His people until they meet the requirements of His holiness. Various Old Testament prophets apply this picture very beautifully to the remnant of Israel who are destined to survive God's judgments and be restored to His favor. For example, in Isaiah 48:10 He says to them:

> (10)   "Behold, I have refined you, but not as silver;
> I have tested you in the furnace of affliction."

Again in Zechariah 13:9:

> (9)   "And I will bring the third part through the fire,
> Refine them as silver is refined,
> And test them as gold is tested.
> They will call on My name,
> And I will answer them;
> I will say, 'They are My people,'
> And they will say, 'The LORD is my God.' "

Metals that pass the test of the furnace are called "refined." These alone have a recognized value. Metals that fail to pass the test are called "rejected." In Jeremiah 6:30 Israel was called "rejected silver," because even the severe, repeated judgments of God had failed to purify them.

In the New Testament, Peter, James, and Paul all alike emphasize that, in the trials through which we pass, it is specifically *our faith* that is being tested. This is the metal of supreme value which cannot be accepted until it has passed the test of fire. At the last supper Jesus warned Peter that he was shortly going to deny his Lord, and in this context He said to him, "But I have prayed for you, that your faith may not fail . . ." (Luke 22:32). In view of the impending pressures and of the weaknesses in Peter's own character, his failure in the hour of crisis was inevitable. Nothing could prevent that. But even so, all would not be lost. The way would still be open for him to return and to confess his Lord once more, upon one condition: *that his faith did not fail.*

The same is true for each of us. There will be times of pressure that will seem unendurable. It may be that, like Peter, we will yield and temporarily fail. But all is not lost! There is a way back, upon one condition: *that our faith does not fail.* No wonder then, that faith is called "precious"—infinitely more so than its material counterpart, the "gold which is perishable." So long as we do not abandon our faith under pressure, we will be able to echo the words of Job in his hour of testing and apparent disaster: "But He [God] knows the way I take; When He has tried me, I shall come forth as gold " (Job 23:10).

The Two Kinds of Test

The parable of the sower, related in Matthew 13:3–8, 18–23, describes the response of four different kinds of people to the message of God's word. The seed that fell by the roadside represents people who never received the message into their hearts at all. The seed that fell on good ground represents people who received the message into their hearts and in due course, by faith and obedience, brought forth enduring fruit. But between these two groups Jesus describes two other types of person—represented by the seed that fell on rocky places and by that which fell among thorns. People in both these groups received the message into their hearts but later failed to meet the conditions for producing good, enduring fruit. We may say of both groups, therefore, that they failed to pass the tests to which they were subjected after initially receiving God's word.

What kind of test is represented by each of these two groups? Let us look first at the seed which fell upon rocky places. In Matthew 13:20–21 Jesus says of this type of person:

> (20)   "And the one on whom seed was sown on the rocky places, this is the man who hears the word, and immediately receives it with joy;
>
> (21)   yet he has no root firm in himself, but is only temporary, and when affliction or persecution arises because of the word, immediately he falls away."

The exact words that Jesus uses here are significant. He does not say, *"if* affliction or persecution arises . . ."* but *"when* affliction or persecution

arises . . ." In other words, affliction and persecution
are sure to come, at some time or other, to everyone
who receives God's word. The question for each of us is
not whether we will have to face these things, but
whether our character will have been so formed that we
will come through them victorious, with our faith
intact. For this, we must allow God's word to penetrate
even into the depths of our hearts, bringing everything
into line with His will. There must be no "rocky places"
anywhere within us to resist the application of the word
to every area of our lives.

What about the seed that fell among thorns? In
Matthew 13:22 Jesus says of this type of person:

> (22) "And the one on whom the seed was sown
> among the thorns, this is the man who
> hears the word, and the worry of the
> world, and the deceitfulness of riches
> choke the word, and it becomes unfruit-
> ful."

The test that eliminates people of this type is not
affliction or persecution. On the contrary, it is just the
opposite: worldly cares and riches. The pressures of
human popularity and materialistic success choke out
the truth of God such people have received, so that in
the end it has no effect on their lives. Instead of being
transformed into the likeness of Christ, they become
conformed to the unbelieving, Christ-rejecting world
around them.

Very simply, we may say that these two groups
represent the two types of test to which all believers
may expect to be subjected. The first test comes when
things are too hard. The second test comes when things
are too easy. Some people give way under the pressure

of persecution; others give way under the pressure of materialistic success. In the book of Proverbs there is a sentence that applies to each type of person. To those who yield under persecution Solomon says, "If thou faint in the day of adversity, thy strength is small " (Proverbs 24:10, KJV). Concerning those who cannot stand success, Solomon says, "For the ease of the simple shall slay them, and the prosperity of fools shall destroy them" (Proverbs 1:32, KJV Margin). Tragically enough, Solomon himself belonged in this latter category. In spite of all his God-given wisdom, in the end his prosperity made a fool of him and destroyed him.

On the other hand, we see in Moses a man who endured both these tests. For 40 years he enjoyed the wealth and luxury of the Egyptian court, being the probable heir to Pharaoh's throne. But then, when he came to maturity, he turned his back on that whole scene and chose the path of loneliness and apparent failure. This is vividly described in Hebrews 11:24–25:

> (24) By faith Moses, when he had grown up, refused to be called the son of Pharaoh's daughter;
>
> (25) choosing rather to endure ill-treatment with the people of God, than to enjoy the passing pleasures of sin.

For the next 40 years Moses underwent the affliction test. He was an exile from his people, a nonentity in the eyes of the world, tending a flock of sheep for his father-in-law on the farthest edge of a barren wilderness.

Yet, when Moses had finally passed both these tests, at the age of 80, he emerged as the God-appointed deliverer and leader of his people. What a striking example of the words already quoted from James 1:4:

"And let endurance have its perfect result, that you may be perfect and complete, lacking in nothing."

The Two Impostors

In his famous poem entitled "If," Rudyard Kipling says something penetratingly true concerning success and failure:

If you can meet with Triumph and Disaster,
And treat those two *impostors* just the same . . .

Whether we call them success and failure, or triumph and disaster, Kipling's description of them is correct—they are both *impostors.* Neither of them is what it seems to be; neither is permanent.

Fortunately we have been given a perfect example of how to deal with these two impostors. No one ever met them more fully or exposed their pretentious claims more effectively than Jesus Himself. He experienced moments of unparalleled success, as when the whole multitude cast their garments in the road before Him and welcomed Him as God's prophet into Jerusalem. Likewise, He experienced moments of total failure, as when, one week later, the same multitude cried out "Crucify Him! Crucify Him!" while his closest friends and followers all forsook Him. Yet Jesus was never unduly elated by success or cast down by failure. Through both alike, He was motivated by one supreme purpose—to do His Father's will and to finish the work His Father had given Him to do. This purpose, unswervingly pursued, carried Him victorious through both kinds of test—success and failure alike.

In Hebrews 12:1-2 the writer first challenges us with

the record of the Old Testament believers whose faith overcame every kind of test and then sets Jesus before our eyes as the final, perfect pattern of endurance and ultimate victory:

(1)   Therefore, since we have so great a cloud of witnesses surrounding us, let us also lay aside every encumbrance, and the sin which so easily entangles us, and let us run with endurance the race that is set before us,

(2)   fixing our eyes on Jesus the author and perfecter of faith, who for the joy set before Him endured the cross, despising the shame, and has sat down at the right hand of the throne of God.

As we follow this exhortation and make Jesus our pattern, we discover that He is in truth both "the author and the perfecter of our faith." He who by His grace began the work in each of us will likewise by His grace complete it. His victory becomes the guarantee of ours. All He requires is that we keep our eyes fixed upon Him.

Summary

Scripture warns us clearly that our faith will be subjected to severe tests. These are necessary to prove its genuineness and to develop strong Christian character in us.

Paul lists four results of such testing: first, perseverance (or endurance); second, proven character; third, hope (a strong, serene, confident expectation of good); fourth, God's love filling our hearts. Finally, testing brings us into a relationship with God where we find our highest satisfaction in nothing and in no one but Himself.

James and Peter likewise teach that tribulation is a necessary part of our total Christian experience. Peter compares the tests we undergo to the fire used by a refiner to purify gold and give it the highest possible value, a figure which is also applied by the Old Testament prophets to God's dealings with Israel.

Paul, James, and Peter all alike assure us emphatically that once we understand the purpose of our tribulations, we will embrace them with joy. Even if we fail temporarily under extreme pressure, we must never give up our faith.

Testing takes two main forms: the first when things are too hard; the second when things are too easy. Moses is an example of a man who endured both these tests and finally emerged as the God-appointed leader of his people. However, the supreme example of dealing with both success and failure is Jesus Himself. As we follow His example, He brings our faith to full maturity.

Chapter Ten

The Measure of Faith

A practical study of faith in the Christian life must take into account the teaching of Paul in Romans 12:1–8 on "the measure of faith":

(1) I urge you therefore, brethren, by the mercies of God, to present your bodies a living and holy sacrifice, acceptable to God, which is your spiritual [or logical] service of worship.

(2) And do not be conformed to this world, but be transformed by the renewing of your mind, that you may prove what the will of God is, that which is good and acceptable and perfect.

(3) For through the grace given to me I say to every man among you not to think more highly of himself than he ought to think; but to think so as to have sound judgment, as God has allotted to each a measure of faith.

(4) For just as we have many members in one

body and all the members do not have the same function,

(5) so we, who are many, are one body in Christ, and individually members one of another.

(6) And since we have gifts that differ according to the grace given to us, let each exercise them accordingly: if prophecy, according to the proportion of his faith;

(7) if service, in his serving; or he who teaches, in his teaching;

(8) or he who exhorts, in his exhortation; he who gives, with liberality; he who leads, with diligence; he who shows mercy, with cheerfulness.

Paul opens this chapter with words, "I urge you therefore . . . " Someone has remarked that when we come across a "therefore" in the Bible, we need to find out what it's *there for*! In this case the "therefore" refers back to all that Paul has been saying in the previous eleven chapters of Romans. In chapters 1 through 8 he has explained how Christ, through His death on the cross, has made a complete and final atonement for sin and all its evil consequences. In chapters 9 through 11 he deals with the stubbornness and blindness of Israel, God's people under the Old Covenant, and with the infinite grace and forbearance that God continues to show toward them.

Having thus unfolded God's mercy toward both Jew and Gentile, Paul says, "Therefore . . . " In the light of all that God has done for all of us, what is our "spiritual—or logical—service"? ("Logical" is the alternative translation offered in the margin for "spiritual.") What is the very least that God can ask of us? It is that we offer Him "our bodies a living and holy sacrifice"—that we lay ourselves totally and without reserve upon God's altar. When Paul says "a *living* sacrifice," he is contrasting our sacrifice with the sacrifices made under the Old Covenant. In those the body of the animal offered in sacrifice was first killed, then placed upon the altar. Under the New Covenant, each one of us is required to place his body just as totally and finally at God's disposal, but with one difference—our body is not killed. It is left alive, to serve God in life, rather than by death.

This offering of our body to God as a living sacrifice represents a total surrender to Him. It opens up the way to a series of steps that leads us into the very center of God's will and provision. The first step is that we begin to change our whole life-style. We cease to be "conformed to this world." We are "transformed." This transformation does not proceed from a set of rules governing our external conduct in matters such as food, dress, ornament, entertainment, etc. It originates from an inner change in our minds. We are "renewed in our minds." Our whole range of attitudes, values, and priorities is adjusted.

Earlier, in Romans 8:7, Paul has told us that "the carnal mind is enmity against God: for it is not subject to the law of God . . . " (KJV). The "carnal mind" describes the way that it has become natural for all of us to think, as a result of our sin and rebelliousness. This mind is actually *at enmity with God.* In human relationships, a person never reveals to an enemy things that are important or precious to him. So it is with God. As long as our minds remain at enmity with Him, there are many precious and wonderful things that He will not reveal to us. But once our minds are reconciled to God by our act of surrender, they are no longer at enmity with Him, but become progressively "renewed" by the Holy Spirit.

To our renewed mind God can begin to reveal His "will"—the special plan that He has for the lives of each one of us. God's will is unfolded in three successive phases, as our minds become more and more fully renewed. In the first phase, God's will is "good"; we discover that He wants only what is good for us. In the second phase, God's will is "acceptable"; the better we understand it, the more ready we are to accept it. In the third phase, God's will is "perfect"; it is complete, all-embracing, making total provision for every area of our lives.

With our minds thus renewed, we do not "think more highly of ourselves than we ought to think." We cease to be proud, self-seeking, self-assertive. We are no longer open to flights of fancy and self-deception. We become sober and realistic; we cultivate "sound judgment." We begin to assimilate the mind of Jesus who said to the Father, "Not My will, but Thine be done." God's plans and purposes are now more important than our own.

This leads to the next discovery: God has dealt to each one of us a specific "measure of faith." It is not for us to determine how much faith we should have. God has already measured this for us and allotted to each of us just that amount which we need. But what standard does God use to measure how much faith we need?

Paul's answer is to explain how the Body of Christ functions: "For just as we have many members in one body and all the members have not the same function, so we who are many, are one body in Christ, and individually members one of another" (Romans 12:4–5). As Christians together we make up one complete "Body." In this Body, each one of us is a particular member, with a specific place and a specific function. One is a nose, another an ear. Another is a hand, yet another is a foot. And so on.

In 1 Corinthians 12:12—28 Paul deals more fully with the concept of the Body and its members. He says that it is God who has "placed the members, each one of them, in the body, *just as He desired*" (verse 18). None of us can choose his own place or function in the Body. All we can do is find and fill the place which God has appointed to us. To do this, as we have already said, requires a "renewed mind."

Paul goes on to point out that, as members of one Body, we are all interdependent. We need each other. None of us is free to do just as he pleases, without regard to the other members. "And the eye cannot say to the hand, 'I have no need of you,' or again the head to the feet, 'I have no need of you' " (verse 21). The head is the highest member, typifying Christ Himself (see Ephesians 4:15). The feet are the lowest members, at the opposite end of the Body. And yet the head needs the feet and cannot do without them. In the light of this we see more clearly why Paul says that to find our place in the Body we must not think too highly of ourselves, but must learn to be sober and realistic.

The picture of the Body and its members enables us to understand what Paul means by the "measure of faith." Each of us is a member in the Body with a specific function. To fulfill our function, we need a specific "measure of faith." The type and amount of faith needed by each member varies. An eye needs "eye faith." A hand needs "hand faith." A foot needs "foot faith." This measure of faith is not interchangeable. The faith that enables a hand to function will not do for a foot. The faith that enables an eye to function will not do for an ear. Each member must have its own appropriate and specific "measure of faith."

Once we have found our appointed place in the Body and we are functioning there with our appointed "measure of faith," we are ready for the next phase of God's provision for us—that is, "gifts" (Greek *charismata*). "And since we have gifts that differ according to the grace given to us, let each exercise them accordingly: if prophecy, according to the proportion of his faith . . ." (Romans 12:6). In addition to prophecy, Paul goes on to name six other gifts: service; teaching; exhorting; giving; leading; showing mercy. This is by no means an exhaustive list of all possible gifts *(charismata)*, but simply a selection to show the kind of variety that is available.

An important principle is here established: *placement and function in the Body come before gifts.* Many Christians are unduly preoccupied with gifts and ministries. They fasten their minds on certain gifts of their own choosing. Usually these tend to be somewhat spectacular, such as gifts of healings or miracles, or the ministry of an apostle or an evangelist. It is true that in 1 Corinthians 12:31 Paul tells us to "earnestly desire the greater gifts." But it is significant that he does not tell us which are "the greater gifts." There is no absolute standard. The value of gifts is relative to our place in the Body. The gifts which enable me to fulfill my God-appointed function best are, for me, "the greater gifts."

Christians who are unduly preoccupied with exciting or spectacular gifts have not heeded Paul's warning to cultivate "sound judgment." Our first responsibility is not to decide what gifts we would like to have; it is to find our place in the Body of Christ. This in turn will determine the type of gifts we will need in order to function there effectively. Experience indicates that once a Christian has settled the question of place and function, the needed gifts come into operation almost spontaneously, without undue effort or striving.

We may now summarize Paul's teaching in Romans 12:1–8. In the light of the unfathomable grace and mercy God has shown to each of us through Christ, our logical response requires that we go through the following successive steps:

(1)   We first present our bodies as a "living sacrifice" to God.

(2)   Through this act of surrender our minds become progressively "renewed" by the Holy Spirit.

(3)   As the outward expression of this change in our minds, our whole life-style begins to change—we are "transformed."

(4)   With our renewed minds we are able to find out in experience the will of God for our lives on three ascending levels: first, as "good"; second, as "acceptable"; third, as "perfect."

(5)   God's will, proved in experience, fits us into our appointed place as a member in the Body and enables us to function there.

(6)   We thus discover that God has given to us a "measure of faith" exactly proportioned to our place and function in the Body—"ear" faith if we are to be an ear, "eye" faith if we are to be an eye.

(7)   As we function in our appointed place with our appointed measure of faith, the "gifts" that we need come into operation.

In chapter 6 we examined Paul's statement in Romans 10:17 that "faith cometh by hearing, and hearing by the word of God." How does this relate to Paul's teaching, here in Romans 12:3–5, that God has allotted to each of us a specific measure of faith, directly related to our appointed place and function in the Body of Christ?

The answer, I believe, is this: "hearing" serves a Christian in the same way as radar serves an airplane. The more sensitive we become to the radar of God's *rhema*—the special word that He speaks to each of us personally—the more surely and easily will we be guided to our appointed place and function in the Body of Christ. Finding our place is like the airplane landing accurately on the runway. "Hearing" is the radar that brings us in exactly where God wants us. Thereafter, as we continue to hear each new *rhema* that comes to us from God, we are kept in our place and enabled to function there effectively.

The fact that God has allotted each of us a specific measure of faith should not be taken to imply that our faith remains static. On the contrary, as our ability to function effectively in the Body grows, our faith grows in proportion. More effective function requires increased faith. Conversely, increased faith produces more effective function. Always, however, there is a fixed relationship between faith and function.

Seen in this light, faith is not some kind of commodity that we can buy or barter in the market places of religion. Rather, it is the expression of a relationship with God, the outcome of an act of surrender that brings us into harmony with God's plan for our lives. As we continue in submission and obedience to God, our faith enables us to take the place and fulfill the function that God has ordained for us. This faith is extremely personal, a specific measure allotted to each one of us. "My" faith will not work for you; "your" faith will not work for me. Each of us must have his own "measure of faith" which fits his individual function in the Body.

While I was still a fairly young Christian, I remember being tremendously impressed by the faith that I saw demonstrated in the life of a more mature believer, one who had made great sacrifices for the Lord and had achieved great successes. Almost without thinking I said one day, "Lord, I don't believe that I could ever have faith like that." Unexpectedly, the Lord gave me a clear, practical answer: "You can't have faith like that because you don't need it! I have not asked you to do what that other person has done." Ever since, I have been grateful for the lesson I learned at that time: *the faith that God gives is proportionate to the task that He asks us to perform.*

Later in my ministry I came across many Christians who obviously had not learned this lesson. They were constantly pleading and struggling for faith, and yet they never seemed to have enough. There was an obvious lack of harmony between their faith and what they were seeking to do. I became convinced that in most cases it was not that God had not given them enough faith. It was that their faith was being misdirected. They were applying it to a task of their own choosing, not to the task which God had actually appointed for them.

Imagine a foot trying to function with a glove on, or a hand with a shoe on. Obviously neither will work properly. There may not necessarily be anything wrong with any of the four things involved: the foot, the hand, the glove, or the shoe. Individually, each may be good and workable. But they are wrongly related to one another. A hand that puts a shoe on and wants to do the work of a foot will be awkward and unsuccessful, as will a foot that puts on a glove and tries to act like a hand.

But when the hand puts on the glove and the foot puts on the shoe, harmony is restored and success is achieved. So it is with the faith that God gives. It fits the member that He appoints—as a glove fits a hand or a shoe fits a foot.

In Hebrews chapter 4 the writer speaks about believers entering into their inheritance. He says, "For we who have believed enter that rest . . ." (verse 3). Faith should bring us into rest. Once we have found our place in our God-given inheritance, we should know a deep, untroubled peace within. There may be much hard work, much pressure and opposition, but in the midst of it all there is inward rest. Continual effort and striving almost certainly indicate that we have not yet found our God-appointed place and function. We are still fumbling, like a hand in a shoe—or stumbling, like a foot in a glove.

A little further on in chapter 4 of Hebrews the writer says, "Let us therefore be diligent to enter that rest . . ." (verse 11). Diligence is required. There is no room for laziness or indifference in the Christian life. But we need to understand the goal to which our diligence should be directed. We are not exhorted, primarily, to acquire faith. We are exhorted to find our place in our inheritance—the very place in the Body for which God has appointed us. Once we have succeeded in finding this, we shall be able to function there without continued struggle or effort, as easily as a foot walks or a hand handles.

Summary

Effective Christian service begins with an act of surrender whereby we present our bodies to God as a "living sacrifice." This in turn leads to a change in our whole way of thinking. Our minds are "renewed." Our total range of attitudes, values, and priorities is progressively adjusted. God's plans and purposes take precedence over our own.

With our "renewed mind" we are able to see ourselves and other Christians as being each of us individual members of one Body. This requires that our first priority should be to find the place and fulfill the function in that Body which God has appointed for us. As we succeed in this, we discover that God has allotted to each of us individually just that "measure of faith" which our place and function require.

Functioning thus with our appointed faith in our appointed place, we become open to the exercise of the particular gifts *(charismata)* that are most needful. These are, for us, "the greater gifts."

If, however, we are continually striving after faith or gifts, this is usually an indication that we have not yet found our appointed place in the Body. Once we have found our place, there is God-given harmony between our function, our faith, and our gifts.

Chapter Eleven

Faith Undoes the Fall

In this closing chapter we will approach the subject of faith from still another angle. We will see that biblical faith, as God imparts it and as it works in our lives, undoes the effects of the fall.

Scripture reveals that man was created in perfection, but fell from that condition by a transgression for which he was accountable to God. However, God was not content to leave man in his fallen condition. Rather, from that point onward, Scripture unfolds a magnificent theme of redemption. It is the story of how God buys man back for Himself by the death of Christ on the cross and how He works out man's restoration, changing his nature and his ways to bring him back into God's original purpose. The key to this process of restoration is *faith*. In other words, the redemptive effect of exercising faith is to reverse the results of the fall.

Faith, Speech, and Creativity

To understand this fully, we must consider the nature of man, the steps which led to his fall, and the essence of the temptation to which he yielded. Then we will see how faith reverses that. The original picture of man as God created him is found in Genesis 1:26: "Then God said, 'Let Us make man in Our image, according to Our likeness . . .' " As we follow this theme on through Scripture, we discover that the "likeness" between God and man has various different aspects.

In this chapter we will concentrate on one aspect of the divine nature—seldom mentioned, but extremely significant—which has its counterpart in the nature of man: *the ability to exercise faith.* Faith is a part of God's own eternal nature. His creative ability proceeds out of His faith. All that He does, He does by faith. Furthermore, His faith finds its expression in the words that He speaks. His words are the channels of His faith and therefore the instruments of His creative ability.

The effective power of God's faith in His own word is forcefully expressed in Ezekiel 12:25. Here the Lord declares: "For I the LORD shall speak, and whatever word I speak will be performed." The introductory phrase "I the LORD" indicates that what follows is part of the eternal, unchanging nature of God. When God says something, it happens. Such is His faith in His own word.

There is a feature of the Hebrew language which vividly illustrates this fact about God and His word. Old Testament Hebrew contains one word—*dabar*—which can equally well be translated as "word" or "thing." Only the context indicates which translation is preferable. Often both are implied. This helps us to understand that God's *words* are *things.* When God speaks a word with His faith, that *word* becomes a *thing.*

Earlier in chapter 6 of this book we saw that the same also is true of the Greek word *rhema* used in the New Testament. God's *rhema*—His spoken word—proceeding out of His faith contains within it the power to fulfill whatever is spoken.

In Hebrews 11:3 we are told that the whole universe was brought into being by the creative power of God's faith in His own word: "By faith we perceive that the universe was fashioned by the word of God, so that the visible came forth from the invisible" (NEB). Behind the entire visible universe, faith discerns one supreme originating cause that is invisible—the word of God. Thus human faith recognizes the outworking of divine faith.

In chapter 3, dealing with the gift of faith, we referred to Psalm 33, verses 6 and 9, where David graphically depicts this process of creation by the spoken word of God:

> (6) By the word of the LORD the heavens were made, And by the breath of His mouth all their host.
>
> (9) For He spoke, and it was done; He commanded, and it stood fast.

In Genesis 1:3 we are given a specific example of how this worked: "Then God said, 'Let there be light'; and there was light." When God spoke the *word* "light," the *thing* "light" was manifested. God's spoken *word* came forth as a *thing*.

Thus we arrive at three conclusions about faith that help us to understand its unique power and importance. First, faith is part of the eternal nature of God. Second, faith is the creative power by which God brought the universe into being. Third, God's faith is expressed and made effective by the words that He speaks.

Because God created man with the ability to exercise faith, we find also in man the other two abilities which are related to faith: the ability to create, and the ability to speak. It is significant that both these abilities, which man shares with God, also distinguish man from the animals.

By his very nature man has creative ability. He can envision something that has never actually existed; then he can plan it and bring it into being. This distinguishes him from all known animals. A bird, for example, can build a marvellously complex nest, but it does so by instinct. A bird cannot envision something that has never existed, plan it, and bring it into being. Man can. In this sense, man is continually creating.

Linked with man's creative ability is man's ability to speak. Without this, man would never be able to formulate and express his creative purposes. Man's capacity for intelligent, articulate speech is not shared by any known animals. It is a distinctive aspect of man's likeness to God.

We see, then, that man, as originally created, shares three related aspects of God's own nature: the ability to exercise faith; the ability to speak; the ability to create.

Satan's Assault on Faith

Because God has shared with man His ability to exercise faith, He requires him to do so. Consequently, when God created man, He placed him in a situation where faith was needed. The record of Scripture makes it clear that God, as a Person, did not remain permanently present with Adam in the garden. Instead, He left him with a substitute for His personal presence—*His word*. In chapter 1 we have already seen that faith relates us to two invisible realities—God and His word. This was the type of relationship in which Adam found himself. He had been in direct personal contact with

God, but when God was no longer present as a Person in the garden, Adam was obligated to relate to God through the word which He had left with him.

This word is recorded in Genesis 2:15—17:

> (15)   Then the LORD God took the man and put him into the garden of Eden to cultivate it and keep it.
>
> (16)   And the LORD God commanded the man, saying, "From any tree of the garden you may eat freely;
>
> (17)   but from the tree of the knowledge of good and evil you shall not eat, for in the day that you eat from it you shall surely die."

Verses 16 and 17 contain the words that God actually spoke to Adam. They fall into three sections: first, a permission; second, a prohibition; third, a warning. The permission: "From any tree of the garden you may eat freely . . ." The prohibition: "But from the tree of the knowledge of good and evil you shall not eat . . ." Finally, the warning: " . . . for in the day that you eat from it you shall surely die." That was God's threefold word to Adam: permission, prohibition, and warning.

As long as man remained rightly related to God through His word, he was blessed and secure. Satan could not touch him. But Satan was determined to alienate man from God and deprive him of His blessings. With characteristic craftiness, he did not begin by directly challenging Adam's relationship to God. Rather, he sought to undermine God's word to Adam. Furthermore, he approached Adam through the "weaker vessel"—Eve.

The initial encounter between Satan and Eve is described in Genesis 3:1—3:

(1)   Now the serpent was more crafty than any beast of the field which the LORD God had made. And he said to the woman, "Indeed, has God said, 'You shall not eat from any tree of the garden'?"

(2)   And the woman said to the serpent, "From the fruit of the trees of the garden we may eat;

(3)   but from the fruit of the tree which is in the middle of the garden, God has said, 'You shall not eat from it or touch it, lest you die.' "

In his strategy to deceive Eve, Satan did not begin by directly denying the word of God—that would have been too obvious! He began by merely questioning it: "Indeed, has God said . . .?" I believe that Eve lost the battle the moment she entertained that question. If we are to retain a right relationship with God, there are some questions to which we must simply close our minds. But Eve trusted in her own judgment. She felt she had the ability to match that charming, intelligent serpent who approached her in the garden. The root of her error was self-confidence.

The next stage of Satan's strategy is recorded in Genesis 3:4: "And the serpent said to the woman, 'You surely shall not die!' " Having first entertained the question, Eve no longer had power to resist the denial.

However, Satan's strategy was not yet complete. To understand his final objective, we need to remind ourselves of two conclusions that we reached in chapter 5. First, the ultimate object of true faith is God Himself. If we ever lose faith in God as a Person, we will eventually give up our faith in His word. Second, if we always had unquestioning faith in God's goodness, God's wisdom, and God's power to provide, there would never be any motive to sin. Satan operated according to these principles. By this time he had succeeded in undermining Eve's faith in God's word. Now he went on to undermine her faith in God Himself. He achieved this by saying, "For God knows that in the day you eat from it your eyes will be opened, and you will be like God, knowing good and evil" (Genesis 3:5).

Taken in their context, Satan's words were aimed at discrediting God's motives in His dealings with Adam and Eve. They insinuated that God was an arbitrary despot, seeking to keep them, through their ignorance, in a state of unmerited inferiority. We might paraphrase Satan's charge against God as follows: "Do you really think that God loves you? Do you think He wants fellowship with you? *No!* Don't you know He's just got you in this garden to keep you under His control? You're really not much better off than slaves. Now, if you were to eat of that tree, things would be different! You wouldn't have to depend on God any longer; you'd be just like God."

This was the final persuasion that broke Eve's relationship with God. She had already given up her confidence in God's word. Now she gave up her confidence in God Himself. Instead of seeing all around her the visible evidence of the love and goodness of the God whom she could not see, she began to accept Satan's dark, cynical picture of God as an arbitrary despot whose purpose was to keep her and her husband in a state of inferiority far below their real potential. Through eating of the forbidden tree, their innate potential for equality with God would be instantly released! Could there be any higher motive than the desire to be like God?

Eve's capitulation is recorded in Genesis 3:6:

(6)   When the woman saw that the tree was good for food, and that it was a delight to the eyes, and that the tree was desirable to make one wise, she took from its fruit and ate; and she gave also to her husband with her, and he ate.

The key word here is "saw." Eve "*saw* that the tree . . . " The word indicates a transition from one realm to another. At this point, Eve abandoned her faith in the invisible realm of God and His word. Instead, she was moved by what she *saw*. She began to rely on her physical senses. She came down from the realm of faith to the realm of the senses. In this lower realm, the tree had three features that attracted her: it was good for food; it was a delight to the eyes; it was desirable to make one wise.

The Nature of Temptation

In 1 John 2:15—16 the apostle lists the three basic forms of temptation:

(15)   Do not love the world, nor the things in the world. If any one loves the world, the love of the Father is not in him.

(16)   For all that is in the world, the lust of the flesh and the lust of the eyes and the boastful pride of life, is not from the Father, but is from the world.

The sensual world, in God's terminology, is made up of three elements: the lust of the flesh; the lust of the eyes; and the boastful pride of life. In Scripture the word "lust" usually denotes a strong desire which has become perverted and harmful and which does not submit to God's standards of righteousness. The first two forms of temptation, listed here by John, are desires of this kind that affect man through his physical senses. The third form of temptation appeals to man's ego, or soul. The "boastful pride of life" is that inner urge in man which refuses to acknowledge his dependence upon God, but seeks to exalt himself. It finds expression in such phrases as: "I can manage my own life . . . I don't need to depend on God . . . Why should I be inferior?"

When Jesus was in the wilderness, He was confronted by Satan with each of these three temptations (see Luke 4:1–13). Satan tempted Him to make stones into bread— *the lust of the flesh.* Then he showed Him all the kingdoms of the world with their power and glory— *the lust of the eyes.* Finally, Satan tempted Jesus to cast Himself down from the pinnacle of the temple, thus performing a miracle on His own initiative that would glorify Himself, without submitting to the Father's will or seeking the Father's glory. That represented *the boastful pride of life.*

There are some interesting points of comparison between the temptation of Adam and the temptation of Jesus (who in 1 Corinthians 15:45 is called "the last Adam"). Adam encountered his temptation in a beautiful garden, surrounded by every evidence of God's loving provision. Jesus encountered His temptation in a barren wilderness, with no companions but the wild beasts (see Mark 1:13). Adam succumbed to his temptation by *eating;* Jesus overcame His temptation by *fasting.* The implications of this comparison are profound!

Returning to Satan's encounter with Eve, we observe that the tree presented her likewise with the three basic forms of temptation. It appealed to her appetite—*the lust of the flesh*. It appealed to her eyes—*the lust of the eyes*. It appealed to her ego with the promise that it would make her wise and thus set her free from dependence on God—*the boastful pride of life*.

In its essence, sin is not doing something wrong. *Sin is the desire to be independent of God.* Whenever this desire appears in us, it spells spiritual danger. In Eve's case, the means by which she hoped to achieve her independence was *knowledge*—the knowledge of good and evil. This is one means by which people commonly seek independence from God. Others are wealth or fame or power. One of the subtlest of all is *religion*. We can become so religious that we no longer need God.

Motivated by her desire for independence, Eve transferred her confidence from God's word to her own senses. As a result she quickly succumbed to the tree's threefold temptation and partook of its fruit. Then she enticed her husband into doing the same and both of them together were alienated from God by their disobedience.

In the light of the foregoing analysis of Genesis 3:1–6, we are now in a position to sum up the nature of temptation. Faith in the invisible realm of God and His word is both original and natural for man; unbelief is perverted and unnatural. Temptation alienates man from his natural faith in God and His word. Instead, it appeals to man through his physical senses. Traced to its roots, every temptation is a temptation to unbelief. The *motive* which it exploits is the desire to be independent of God. The *result* which it produces is disobedience against God.

Faith Is the Antidote

Faith works in exactly the opposite direction to temptation. Faith requires man to renounce both his confidence in his senses and the ambition of his ego to exalt himself in independence of God. On the contrary, faith reasserts the supremacy of the invisible realm of God and His word and requires man's ego to humble himself and acknowledge his dependence upon God. Thus faith undoes the effects of man's fall and opens the way for him to return into his original relationship with God.

Confronted with God's requirement of faith on the one hand and with the claims of his senses on the other, man finds himself in a dilemma, caught in a tension between two opposing forces. The two opposite poles of this tension are set forth in Habakkuk 2:4: "Behold, his soul which is lifted up is not upright in him; but the just shall live by his faith" (KJV). As we have already noted, the second half of this verse is quoted three times in the New Testament, providing the scriptural basis for justification by faith, rather than by works. However, we can only see the full scope of the dilemma when we set the two halves of the verse over against one another, viewing them as opposites, each of which excludes the other.

It is important to see that the first half of the verse describes man's soul in its rebellion against God. The Jewish version reads, "Behold, his soul is puffed up, it is not upright in him . . ." This corresponds to what John calls "the boastful pride of life." We might paraphrase it, "The soul that exalts itself becomes perverted." Man's ego, seeking to exalt himself, rejects the claims of God and His word, but prefers instead to trust his own senses and to strive after independence from God.

The second half of the verse depicts the opposite alternative. The man who makes faith his basis for living humbles himself before God, accepting God's word as his standard and rejecting confidence in himself and his senses. The senses appeal to man's independent, self-exalting ego, but faith humbles man's ego, saying in effect: "You are *not* independent. You must depend on God. You can trust your senses only insofar as they agree with God's word. Your final standard of right and wrong, of truth and error, is not what your senses tell you but what God says in His word."

Thus faith cuts away the ground on which the fall took place. The fall made man captive to the sense realm: "Eve *saw* that the tree was good . . . " It exalted man's ego: "You will be like God." All that self-exaltation must be undone if we are to live the life of righteousness that is pleasing to God. How is it to be undone? By the faith principle. Faith rejects both the dominion of the senses and the boastful, self-exalting pride of the soul.

In Romans 3:27 Paul points out that true faith is incompatible with pride: "Where then is boasting? It is excluded. By what kind of law? Of works? No, but by a law of faith." Any kind of religious feeling or activity that leaves room for man's independent, self-exalting egotism is not the expression of valid, scriptural faith.

So there are two ways of living. One in which man rejects dependence upon God, but trusts in himself and his senses. The other in which man renounces confidence in himself and his senses, but trusts in that which his senses cannot comprehend—God and His word. By weaning us away from self and the sense realm, faith brings us back to the principle of righteous-

ness which is based on trust in God and His word and
which alone enables us to live a life that is pleasing to
God.

FAITH IS THE ANTIDOTE TO THE FALL.

Summary

Faith is part of the eternal nature of God. Through
His word, spoken in faith, He created the entire
universe. As part of his likeness to God, man shares
three aspects of the divine nature: the ability to exercise
faith; the ability to speak; and the ability to create.

Having created man with the ability to exercise faith,
God placed him in a situation where he needed to do so.
Adam in the garden did not continue to relate directly
to God as a Person. Instead, he related to God through
the word which God left him—the threefold word of
permission, prohibition, and warning.

To alienate Adam from God, Satan approached him
indirectly through the "weaker vessel"—Eve. He began
by undermining Eve's confidence in God's word,
through first questioning it and then directly denying it.
Then he went on to undermine her confidence in God
Himself by suggesting that she and her husband did not
need to remain in a position of inferiority, but could
achieve equality with God by acquiring the knowledge
of good and evil. This desire for independence from
God is the inner motivation that leads to sin.

In this way Eve was persuaded to renounce her
confidence in the invisible realm of God and His word.
She came down instead to the realm of the senses. The
forbidden tree confronted her with the three basic
forms of temptation: the lust of the flesh; the lust of
the eyes; the boastful pride of life. On the lower realm

of the senses, Eve was no longer able to resist the tree's appeal, but succumbed to its temptation and persuaded her husband to do the same.

Faith reverses this process of temptation that led to man's fall. Faith requires man to renounce confidence in his senses and the self-exalting desire of his ego to achieve independence from God, and to reaffirm his final confidence only in the invisible realm of God and His word. Man's destiny is determined by his response to faith's requirement.